creative youth leadership

for adults who work with youth

jan corbett

Judson Press ® Valley Forge

CREATIVE YOUTH LEADERSHIP

Library of Congress Cataloging in Publication Data

Corbett, Jan.
  Creative youth leadership.

  1. Social work with youth.   2. Leadership.
I. Title.
HQ796.C817   301.15'53   77-8950
ISBN 0-8170-0761-X

Cartoons by Doug Brunner.

The name JUDSON PRESS is registered as a trademark in the U.S. Patent Office.
Printed in the U.S.A. ✜

Contents

A Word of Thanks

This book began as a training resource for the Department of Ministry with Youth of the American Baptist Churches, U.S.A. While the author was unaffiliated with the department at the time the book was written, the department staff remained supportive and offered a helpful critique of each chapter. In addition, the models of leadership which they have personally provided have greatly influenced the content of the book. Thanks to John (Bud) Carroll, Ronald Schlosser, Jeffrey Jones, and Marilyn Marston for their time and expertise.

Special thanks to Vergie Gillespie, whose insight and editorial comments have been invaluable in shaping the final manuscript of the book.

j. c.

How to Use This Book

This is a book for youth leaders—new leaders who have never before worked with youth, experienced leaders who want to brush up on their skills, and administrators who want to discover the kinds of skills necessary for effective youth leadership.

If you are a new leader, you will want to use the book as a study guide. It provides a step-by-step design for developing skills in youth leadership. You will begin with a survey of "survival skills"—the skills you will need to have before your first session with youth. These are basic skills which are necessary for all leader responsibilities: leading a discussion, brainstorming, role play, Bible study, research, and worship. When you have mastered these skills, you will be able to lead a group with moderate effectiveness. You can then move on to the more sophisticated skills discussed in the final chapters of the book. You can study the characteristics of youth and learn how groups function. Finally, you can discover ways of continuing your growth as a leader and evaluate the kinds of expectations you might have for results from your leadership.

If you are an experienced leader, the table of contents will be your most important tool. Look up areas in which you are weak or in which you need to develop new skills. Read other sections to review your knowledge of the components of youth leadership.

This book can be used for group training of youth leaders. The chapters are self-contained and each can be the basis for one session in a training event. All of the chapters on skills have examples of the use of the skill (sample role plays, sample brainstorming situations, etc.) which can be practiced in a group training session. The book is designed as a progressive course. Each chapter builds on the chapter preceding it. Here is one way of outlining a training course, using this book as a text:

Unit I: The Basics of Youth Leadership
> Session 1: Motivation and Preparation for Youth Leadership (chapter 1)
> Session 2: Basic Teaching Skills (chapter 2)
> (This could be expanded into sessions dealing with each skill.)
> Session 3: Planning the Learning Session (chapter 3)

Unit II: Understanding Youth
> Session 1: Myths About Youth (chapter 4)
> Session 2: Characteristics of Youth (chapter 5)

Unit III: Skills for the Experienced Youth Leader
> Session 1: A Planning Process (chapter 6)
> Session 2: Understanding Groups (chapter 7)
> Session 3: Teaching Skills (chapter 8)
> (This could be expanded into sessions dealing with each skill.)
> Session 4: Finding and Using Resources (chapter 9)
> Session 5: Choosing Learning Settings (chapter 10)

Unit IV: Problem Clinic
> Session 1: Common Leadership Problems (chapter 11)
> Session 2: The Leader's Expectations (chapter 12)

Section 1
Survival Skills
for the
New Leader

What Do You Do After You Say "Yes"? 1

Effective youth leaders are made—not born. And the "making" often involves a great deal of time, extensive training, and a high level of commitment. Professionals study full time for up to three years to prepare for these responsibilities. Most lay persons, however, do not have this kind of time to invest either in training or in the responsibility itself. They must work, raise families, participate in Rotary Clubs, drive in car pools, go mountain climbing, and do all of the other things that make them the interesting, fulfilled, contributing members of society who make good youth leaders.

Youth leadership is only one of the many activities in which lay persons are involved. And, because their employment and families take most of their time, youth leadership is often relegated to marginal time. How can they possibly do an effective job? How can they do any more than lecture about the faith or keep horseplay to a minimum? How can they develop meaningful relationships and see real growth take place?

Because I began youth leadership as a lay person, moved to the professional level, and then spent many hours training lay persons in youth leadership, I have pondered this dilemma for many years. And I have come to the conclusion that there are ways of becoming proficient youth leaders when limited time is available, if approached one step at a time. I believe there are certain basic skills which I have called "survival skills" (a term actually coined by national youth leader Bud Carroll). By mastering these basic skills, motivated lay youth leaders can teach a class or lead a group with moderate effectiveness. Then, if they move on from this point to refine these skills and develop their own creativity, they can become very effective youth leaders. This is a process that may take several years, depending on the time and training available, but it results in the kind of youth leadership which is needed in the church.

This book is based on the above step-by-step process. The first section outlines the basic "survival skills." We then move on to a more in-depth look at relationships between youth and adults and to developing more personal creativity in leadership. The final chapters cover some more sophisticated leader skills. We close with a look at some common problems encountered in youth leadership and some realistic results.

Perhaps we should say at the outset that the "survival skills" outlined in this section should not be seen as skills which are mastered and then discarded when the lay leader becomes better trained and more creative. They remain the basic skills for all youth leadership. The more experienced leader simply adapts them to fit the needs of the group; he or she supplements them with the use of more sophisticated techniques or resources.

WHEN TO SAY "YES"

With this in mind, let's begin at the beginning. You have just been approached to teach a youth church school class or to be a youth group counselor. In a weak moment, you said "yes." What do you do first?

Wait a minute. Did we say in a weak moment? Better stop to deal with that one. If you agreed to work with youth because: (*a*) no one else would do the job; (*b*) you felt guilty because you were not doing anything in the church; (*c*) your own teenagers are in the group and you feel you should do your share; (*d*) you feel youth today are going down the wrong track and you can set them straight; or for any of a number of negative reasons, you'd better reconsider. This kind of motivation doesn't hold up when the going gets rough. In addition, it might even be harmful to the youth with whom you work. So, before you say yes, consider why you want the position.

Reasons for Saying "Yes"

Some positive reasons for accepting a teaching or counseling job with youth are:

● You are able to relate with youth. You can be your (adult) self with them and accept them as they are. They seem to enjoy being with you.

● You feel comfortable with your own faith, but are not locked into a rigid position. You are open to the kind of questioning and searching most youth experience. You take their questions seriously and are open to insights which you have never considered. You can learn from them as well as teach them.

• You have some skills in teaching and leading groups, or you are willing to develop some basic skills before you begin.

• You understand what youth ministry is all about, and you want to be a part of it. You think youth should be a part of the church—not members in waiting. You want to be their advocate with other adults in the church.

If your reasons for saying "yes" are close to those above, you're more likely to be responding from a positive motivation which will make your job rewarding. Now, where do you begin?

A Leadership Contract

First, it's important to know just what is expected of you. You need to prepare a contract which outlines your responsibilities. That may sound pretty formal. After all, this isn't a job you're being paid for. But it's surprising how many headaches you save by establishing right from the start what is expected of you, even in a voluntary job like teaching a senior high church school class.

Keep in mind that many people in the church have their own ideas about what should be happening in youth ministry. Parents may want their youth to become active members of the church. Older members may feel that there's a future for the church if a lot of senior highs attend the Sunday morning worship service. The minister may want someone to free her or him from working with youth so she or he can meet other responsibilities. The church school superintendent may want to fill a vacant teaching spot. Youth themselves may have a variety of expectations—from digging into some deep theological study to having the kind of close-knit group that supports them in their own search for self, to simply having a good time with their friends.

The person who recruits you should, ideally, provide you with clear-cut directions about what is expected of you. But if this doesn't happen, you may have to develop your own contract, with this person's help. Some sample contracts are in the Appendix, pages 117 and 118.

Your contract should represent the policy of the church in youth ministry. It may differ from some parents' expectations or from those of other church members, but it should fit with the policy developed by your official educational board. For example, some people in the church may expect you to determine the direction the youth group goes, while your church's educational board may expect youth to share in this decision. Other people might expect you to use a curriculum in the church school which they feel is better than that provided by the educational board. Make sure you understand what the position of the board is on this.

You should not have to fight policy battles with members of the church. Policies should be set by the educational board, who should outline your job in such a way that policies are carried out.

BECOMING ACQUAINTED WITH YOUR GROUP

After you have a clear concept of your responsibilities, you are ready to begin. And the starting place is becoming acquainted with your group.

If you have never worked with youth, or you have been away from youth work for a long time, you may want to experiment with youth relationships in a nonthreatening practice session before you approach your own group.

Try spending an afternoon or evening with some teenagers who are not in the group—children of friends, your own children, a younger brother or sister, and their friends. Take the group out for pizza. Spend most of your time listening. Concentrate on the issues that are being discussed. What do you really know about Mr. Robertson who gives such hard exams in earth science? Are you aware of the high school league standing in basketball? What about the use of alcohol among high school students in your town?

After you return home, jot down some notes about the conversation. What did the group talk about? What did they feel strongly about? Did you feel alien to their world? Did you feel that they accepted you as a part of their world? Where did you have trouble entering the conversation? Why?

Next, spend an afternoon with just one teen. Take a friend's teenager to a ball game or to a movie. Try to get to know this one person and to let the teenager know you. Share as much about yourself as this person seems to want to know. Try to encourage the teen to share with you.

Your object in your conversation with a group of teens and with just one teen is to feel comfortable talking with teens. Many adults, especially those with teenagers of their own, find they can only relate to youth on a parent-child basis. They find themselves pointing out what is wrong with the young people's behavior, criticizing their attitudes toward teachers or toward other students, and giving them answers to questions rather than helping them find answers themselves. They notice such things as elbows on the table, slang expressions, and sloppy dress, rather than excited expressions and interesting ideas. Try to think of the youth with whom you talk as friends you would like to get to know better and whom you would like to know you better. Relate to them as you relate to your own friends.

When it comes time actually to meet your class or group, there are some techniques you can use to become better acquainted and to help the group feel at ease with both you and each other. A portion of your first session, or even the entire session, should be devoted to these.

Getting Acquainted Techniques

As the youth enter the room, have everyone make a name tag and have other persons pin them on their **backs.** You should also make a tag.

When everyone has arrived, set a timer for two minutes. Ask everyone (yourself included) to mill around the room looking at name tags and trying to memorize names. **There should be no talking.** When the timer rings, reset it for two minutes and ask everyone to mill around, shaking the hands of everyone they meet, again without talking. On the final round they pull the left ear lobe of everyone they meet, still not talking.

Now, arrange everyone in a circle. Go around the circle and ask the youths to introduce the person on their right without looking at the name tag on the back of the person. Switch chairs and repeat this three times.

Next, divide the group into pairs. (You should also be paired.) Ask the pairs to interview each other, finding out at least one interesting thing they can share with the total group. Come back together in a large group and share what you have found out about each other.

If possible, have refreshments and finish the session with informal sharing.

SUMMARY

In this first chapter we have presented the principle on which this book is based—that effective youth leadership can be developed through a step-by-step process, beginning with what we are calling "survival skills" and moving into more sophisticated skills and more creative leadership.

Before we even accept a leadership position, we need to consider our motivation. We need to be confident that we have some initial skills and be willing to secure the additional skills needed for effective leadership. We need to ask for a clear job description or contract which will outline our responsibilities.

Once we have accepted responsibility for leading a group of youth, we need to become acquainted with them. Then we must move on to developing some basic teaching skills. These teaching skills are outlined in the next chapter.

Survival Teaching Skills 2

Whether you are teaching a class or counseling a youth group, you will need to have some basic knowledge of simple teaching skills. The following are the ones you should carry in your survival kit. Other more sophisticated methods will be discussed later in this book, but the methods described in this chapter will get you through the early sessions with your group and will remain your basic techniques throughout your career as a youth leader.

It is important to note at the outset that these methods cannot be learned by simply reading about them. You will need to practice them over and over until you can use them without thinking about the steps. This practice should ideally be done before you begin working with your group. Try it on your family or friends. Or get together with some other new leaders and practice together.

LEADING A DISCUSSION

Probably the thing you will be called on to do most often is to lead a discussion. Most of us have had some experience with this, but it has not always been successful. Many discussions break down into: a search for the "right" answer, a monologue by a bright student or the teacher, an embarrassed silence, or a few mumbled, one-syllable answers.

To prevent these disastrous results, try the following:

• **Never ask questions which can be answered "yes" or "no."** Ask "why" questions or "what do you think" questions, or questions that call for facts. For example, let's say you are studying the two accounts of the creation in Genesis. Don't ask, "Did God create the world in seven days?" or "Did God put man in charge of the other creatures he created?" Instead, ask, "How long does the account of the creation say God took to create the world? What was the significance of seven days to the Hebrews?" Or ask, "Why do you think two different accounts of the creation are included in Genesis?"

Many new teachers and leaders hesitate to ask questions which get away from facts and get into opinions because they feel they should know all the answers. This is unnecessary, especially in religious discussions. Who has all the answers? Let the group know that you are searching for answers just as they are. Approach the study as a learner along with your students. Show that you value their insights and that they might have some answers you have not yet considered. There is nothing that brings a discussion to a dead end quicker than a teacher who is obviously looking for answers he or she already knows.

● **Try to get students to ask questions of each other.** A good discussion is one in which everyone gets into the act, agreeing and disagreeing with each other and challenging the others to defend their positions. If Judy says, "I think the creation stories are just ways the early Hebrews tried to explain the beginning of the world," you can say, "Herb, how do you feel about that?" When Herb has finished, say, "Does anyone disagree with Herb or Judy?" Try to think of your role as keeping the ball moving. Draw in people who seem to be on the outside. Challenge those whom no one else challenges. Give your own opinion and let it be challenged.

● **Concentrate on feelings.** Getting to the feeling level in a discussion keeps it from being a heady, intellectual exercise. After seeing a movie, ask, "How did that make you feel? Happy? Depressed? Excited? Hopeful? Confused?" Then push to find out why people felt that way. With which character did they identify? Why? Have they had an experience like the one that brought forth these feelings?

Many people answer the question, "How do you feel?" with a statement about what they think. For example, they say, "I feel that it was very unfair to tease that little boy." Push persons to use words that describe their emotions: "I felt horrified when that little boy was teased."

● **Do not be afraid of silence.** Most people need time to think. If there is no immediate response to your question, don't be alarmed. And don't keep talking. Wait a reasonable amount of time before encouraging a response by rephrasing your question.

● **Talk about the high and low points.** When everyone has

participated in an experience together, whether it was a field trip or simply reading a story together, ask everyone to tell what the high point of the experience was. Then ask for the low point. This will allow everyone to review what was meaningful. Respect each person's contribution. There are no "right" or "wrong" high or low points.

• **Use sentence completion questions.** For a change, ask everyone to discuss a reading by completing a sentence. For example, if you have read Psalm 8, ask students to complete the sentence: "When David wrote this psalm, he was feeling _____." Or, "This psalm makes me feel _____." As warned earlier, do not use sentences which can be filled in with correct or incorrect factual data. ("David said man was _____.") This cuts short any discussion.

• **Do not evaluate answers.** Many teachers think they are encouraging students when they say, "That's a good insight" or "That's right." Rather than encouraging a student, it makes the student feel that the answer is subject to teacher approval or disapproval. This may inhibit other students from contributing. Try to feel that you are a part of the group and are contributing like everyone else—not simply accepting or rejecting the contributions group members make.

• **Begin discussions in small groups.** If your group is fairly large and the members are not well acquainted with each other, it may be helpful to break into three's or five's to begin a discussion. It is easier for most people to talk with a small number of people initially. You can then call the small groups together and ask each to report to the larger group. People may then feel free to discuss as a larger group.

BRAINSTORMING

Almost every youth counselor and many youth teachers are called upon to moderate a discussion of what the group is going to do: where they will go on a retreat, what they will use as a theme for a youth worship service, what they will do as a Christmas project, etc. One way of making sure the decision is one in which everyone has a share is to brainstorm the question.

Brainstorming is a very simple process. You simply ask everyone to put out an idea. You make a list of these ideas as they are given, without discarding or discussing any of them. You keep writing down ideas until no more come from the group. Then you go over the list and ask for clarification of any ideas persons do not understand. Next, you put together any ideas that seem similar. Then you ask the group to decide which idea or group of ideas they like the best.

Here's an example. Your group is trying to decide on a place for a retreat. You ask what they want the place to provide. Here is the list they come up with:

Place where we can do our own cooking
Not more than three hours from the church
Fireplace or place for outside bonfire
Cots
Lake for swimming and boating
Place for sleeping bags
Place to play softball
Showers
Place where we can make noise late at night
Indoor bath facilities
Room for large meeting inside
Not very costly

Your next step is to ask for clarification of anything on the list. Someone asks what is meant by "not very costly." Someone else asks what kind of place would be needed to get away by yourself.

You then go through the list and put together the things that fit together. For example, here are some things you might put together:

Sleeping: cots, place for sleeping bags
Facilities: showers, indoor bath facilities, fireplace, place to cook, meeting room, place to make noise late at night
Recreation: swimming, boating, softball, trails for getting away by oneself
Limitations: not costly, not more than three hours from church

Now you ask the group to check the categories they think are most important. They check facilities first and limitations second. You point out that they will have to make a decision about whether they want cots or simply a floor for sleeping bags—or both. You then appoint a committee to search for a retreat facility that meets their needs, in the order of preference they have given. Your list will now look like this:

1. Facilities: meeting room inside, place to cook, fireplace (optional)

2. Limitations: not costly, not more than three hours from church

ROLE PLAY

Role playing has become a standard teaching technique in most church school curricula and in many youth group resources. It helps youth put themselves in the shoes of other persons and experience what it is like to live their faith in relationship with others.

Role playing is actually just playing roles—becoming another person and playing out a situation as that person would play it, without a written script.

You begin with a problem situation which is described in your resource material. Pick out the roles in this situation and describe what each character is like. Ask persons in your group to assume these roles. They spend a few minutes thinking about what their role is like. Then you act out the situation, bringing the problem to some solution. The rest of the group then discusses the various points of view expressed and how effective the solution was.

Here is an example of how this works. Your resource material gives the following situation:

Ann's parents have gone away for the weekend. She is staying home alone and has promised that she will not have any of her friends in. However, on Friday night she goes to a party with her boyfriend, Roger. He brings her home in a van full of other friends. When they reach her home, everything is dark. The driver of the van, Jim, says, "Hey, your folks aren't waiting up for you." Ann says, without thinking, "They're away for the weekend." "Wow!" Jim says, "Just what we've been looking for—a place for a real bash. I've got a six-pack in the back. Let's go."

Discuss the problem faced in this situation. Have someone state it in a sentence or two. Then talk about the characters that are in this role play. In addition to Ann, Roger, and Jim, there are several other friends in the van. Let someone describe what they think each character is like. Then ask people to volunteer to take the roles.

Next, arrange the setting. Role playing can be done without props or a stage, but a few symbolic items add reality. For example, in this role play you may want to use several chairs for the seats in the van. Another chair can mark Ann's house.

Now, get into the role play. Begin with the dialogue given in the situation. Here is one way it *might* go. (This is an example of possible dialogue. Your characters will develop their own dialogue as they play out their roles.)

ANN (*whispers to Roger*): I told my folks I wouldn't have any friends in while they were gone.

ROGER (*whispering back*): Don't worry, I'll see that nothing happens. After all, we owe Jim something for the ride.

JIM: What are you two whispering about? Let's get this stuff inside.

ANN: Jim, you can come in if you want, but don't bring any beer. My folks would really be upset.

JIM: What do you mean, no booze? What's a party without booze? Hey, Roger, where'd you get this child?

ROGER: It's Ann's house, Jim. I think she should say what can happen there. After all, she has to answer to her folks.

JIM: Folks, schmolks. What are you, a mama's girl? Come on, I'll show you how to have a good time. (*Tries to push past Ann.*)

OTHER FRIENDS (*Grab Jim and push him back into the van*): Come on, Jim. Roger's right. It's Ann's house. We can have our own party down at the beach. We don't need a house. We've got this whole van. Are you coming, Roger?

ROGER: Yeah, just let me say good night. (*Ann and Roger part at door.*)

After the role play has been completed, ask the group members who were watching to comment on it. Some questions you might ask are: How did you feel when Ann said the group couldn't bring beer into the house? With whom did you identify at this point? Did you think the ending was satisfactory? Could you think of a better ending? Do you think Ann should have allowed the group in the house even without beer?

Now ask each character to tell how they felt as they played out their role. How did Jim feel when Ann said he could not come in with his six-pack? Is he used to getting his own way? How did Ann feel when Roger went along with Jim? Did Roger feel caught in the middle?

If you have time, you might ask other persons to assume the roles and play out an entirely different solution to the situation.

There are some pitfalls to be aware of in role playing. First, be sure that you use situations with which your group can identify. They must feel that the roles are real and are ones they might actually be called upon to take in a similar situation. Also, be careful that you do not talk out a solution to the problem before the role play begins. The object of role play is for persons to place themselves in the shoes of another person and act as that person might act. Finally, do not cast persons in roles that are similar to ones they actually take in real life. For example, if someone in your group is used to pushing his weight around, don't ask him to play the role of Jim.

BIBLE STUDY

Another "must" for the beginning teacher or counselor is to know how to lead meaningful Bible study. To be effective in this, you must first think through what you want your group to understand as they study the Bible. To put this in a different way, you must think through your own understanding of the Bible and its value in your day-to-day existence.

My own position is that the Bible describes the search of a people for a meaningful relationship with God and the action of God in shaping these people's lives, so that they can live in harmony with each other and with God. By studying the interaction of people with God in the past, we learn how to duplicate this in our own lives.

If we are going to know God as God was known by people in biblical times, we need not only to read the stories of people in the Bible but also to understand their culture, their historical situation, and even the meaning of the ancient texts which have been translated into our language. This is a long and tedious process, and biblical scholars devote whole lifetimes to it. We do not have to repeat their work. We can rely on their findings as reported in commentaries, Bible dictionaries, and Bible atlases. And we can help youth in our groups to use these resources, too. We should always have such resources available when we do Bible study.

Here is an example of the Bible study process:

Let's assume you are studying the types of literary forms used in the Bible and are at the point of learning what parables are. Have the students read the parable of the mustard seed in Matthew 13:31-32. Ask them to define a parable. If they are unable to do this, have someone look up the meaning in a Bible dictionary. Ask: How is a parable different from a short story or historical account? Are parables used today? If so, illustrate this. (Students might consider the use of parables in popular songs.) What are the advantages of using parables? What are the disadvantages?

Then discuss the way Jesus got across universal truth through the use of parables. To understand this, look more closely at the meaning of the parable of the mustard seed. Ask: What universal truth was Jesus explaining? Why did he select the mustard seed; what is unique about this seed and plant? What is this parable saying about the kingdom of God? What does it say to us in our everyday lives?

These questions may be discussed in small groups. Then, as a total group, listen to someone read the interpretation of the parable in a good Bible commentary and ask the group if this gives them any more insight into the meaning. (A good commentary is *The Interpreter's One-Volume Commentary on the Bible,* Nashville: Abingdon Press, 1971.)

Ask the group to write their own parable illustrating the growth of the kingdom of God. With what would they compare it today?

Have group members share their own parables. Ask if they now understand this literary form better.

RESEARCH

Leading your group in research is one of the simpler skills you will have to acquire. The main thing in research is to ask the right questions—ones which will force students to dig for answers. (Refer to the section on discussion for help in formulating these questions.) In addition, you will have to provide the right resources for youth to find answers to their questions.

Here is an example of how a research project might go. Your group is engaged in a study of religious symbols. You begin by having the members list all the symbols they can recall seeing. Then provide them with books on religious symbols and ask them to add other symbols to the list. Put the symbols into categories (crosses, symbols of the Trinity, secret symbols of the early Christian church, symbols of baptism, etc.). Then ask committees to research each symbol category, trying to discover: When did the symbol originate? How has it been used? Has its meaning changed? Where is it used today? What modern symbol might be used to replace it? Reports are made to the entire group, who can ask questions of the committee researching each category.

The temptation in leading research is to give all of the answers yourself. That certainly saves time! However, the project will be much more meaningful if youth do the research themselves. They will learn ten times as much because they have dug out the answers and reported them.

WORSHIP

The final survival skill you will need is the ability to plan and conduct a worship service. Ideally, youth should plan their own worship most of the time. But you will need to know how this is done in order to help them develop their own skill.

It is helpful to use a standard outline in planning a worship service. Here is one outline which is traditionally used:

Opening: acknowledging the presence of God

Period of praise

Period of confession

Meditation: developing new insights into God's action

Commitment: expressing desire to take part in God's action

Closing: moving out into the world where commitment is carried out

This outline can be used with a traditional liturgy in liturgical churches, or you can develop your own content for each part. Here is one way this might be done:

WORSHIP FOR THANKSGIVING

OPENING: Psalm 100:1-2

PERIOD OF PRAISE: Hymn, "All Creatures of Our God and King"

PERIOD OF CONFESSION: Create a litany in which members confess times they might not have expressed their thanksgiving. For example:

Leader: We confess that we often take for granted that we will have food on our tables and more at the corner store.

Group: Help us to be more thankful.

Leader: We confess that we accept the gift of the family car, even when someone else is inconvenienced.

Group: Help us to be more thankful.

(Litanies can be found in most hymnals.)

MEDITATION: Have someone give a brief talk about the meaning of Thanksgiving today, challenging the group not just to say they are thankful but also to express their thanksgiving in their actions.

COMMITMENT: Create a prayer of commitment, expressing thanksgiving, to be prayed in unison by the group.

CLOSING: Hymn, "Spirit of the Living God"

SUMMARY

This chapter has covered some basic teaching skills which

will be needed in any youth leadership situation: leading a discussion, brainstorming, role playing, Bible study, research, and worship.

These are basic skills which each youth leader should be able to use effectively. If you do not presently feel comfortable using any of these techniques, plan to secure some training in them. Many denominations offer regional and national training opportunities. There are a number of training courses available through films and cassettes. An experienced leader in your church may be able to tutor you in some skills.

You can even train yourself. Simply read the information about the skill given in this chapter and then try out the example with your family or a group of friends. Brainstorm on the topic of the location of your family's vacation. Lead a discussion with your friends on a current news topic. Ask some friends to help you do a role play or Bible study.

These are your "survival skills," and you will need to master them before you begin working as a youth leader. And they will remain your basic teaching skills throughout your leadership career.

Planning the Learning Session 3

The final "survival skill" you will need for youth leadership is skill in planning learning sessions. Whether you are teaching a formal church school class or using program materials with a youth group, this skill is a "must."

For your first experience as a youth leader, you should insist that your church provide you with resources which give fairly structured, but educationally sound, session plans. That is, they give step-by-step directions, but the sessions are not simply a lecture followed by discussion; they involve the group in a variety of learning activities and help students reach their own theologically sound understandings.

Most denominational curriculum resources meet this criteria, as do resources for youth groups like *Respond* and *Explore* (published by Judson Press, Valley Forge, Pa.) or the Serendipity Series by Lyman Coleman (published by Word, Inc., Waco, Texas). Your job will be to adapt these plans to your own group. Here are the things to consider.

THE SESSION GOAL

The goal for the session is usually given at the beginning of the plan. Read it over and decide if it is a goal which will interest your group. To make this decision, you should have some knowledge of your group, as suggested in the section about getting to know your group. You may want to invite two or three members of the class or group to plan with you and to ask them to make a decision about the goal.

Write out the goal in your own words or the words of your planning group. Ideally, it should be written as a statement of the behavior you think will be changed. What will actually happen to the learner as a result of this session? What skills will the learner develop? What new attitudes will the learner have? What new information will the learner discover?

CHOOSING ACTIVITIES

Most resource materials provide activities which will enable the average group to meet the goal. You will need to decide whether the activities provided are ones which will help your group achieve the goal as you have rewritten it.

It is helpful to have a group of youth meet with you to select activities and to take responsibility for leading the session. Ask them if the activities are ones to which members of the group will respond. If discussion questions are provided, ask the planning group to revise these questions to reflect interests of your own group. This is illustrated in the sample session below.

EVALUATION

After the session is over, you will want to evaluate whether you met your goal. Meet with your planning group to do this. Most session plans have some evaluation techniques like questionnaires or opportunities for sharing built into the session itself. These enable you to see whether group members have learned any new information, changed their attitudes, or developed new skills. Ask the planning group to go over the evaluation which took place during the session and decide how well your goal was achieved. Then do a more general evaluation. Ask, "Were the activities ones which our group found exciting and useful? Was the topic of interest? What went really well? Why? What flopped? Why?"

This kind of evaluation will help you learn from your successes and mistakes and improve your skill in planning learning sessions.

A SAMPLE SESSION PLAN

Let's take an actual session from *Respond, Volume 4* (Valley Forge: Judson Press, 1975) to illustrate the session planning process.

The session "It's All Right to Fail" has as a goal (or "target" as it is called in *Respond*): "To help youth creatively face their experiences of failure; to help them see that they are not alone; and to help provide some tools for an appropriate response to failure." Do you know what experiences members of your group have had with failure? Have they had any recent experiences? Try to jot down some of the experiences of which you are aware. What resources for dealing with failure do you think they already have? Do they need to learn to handle failure better? If so, this goal is appropriate for your group.

Write out this goal in your own words, rephrasing it in terms of the changes in behavior you expect in group members. For example: Youth will be able to identify ways failure experiences led to their growth.

Bring together a small group to plan the meeting. At this time you will talk about failure experiences—those of members in the group and your own. Out of this discussion should come some questions the group has about dealing with failure. For example, they may ask, "How do you face parents when you bring home an F in geometry? How do you get up the courage to ask another girl out when the first one turns you down? How do you enjoy the neighborhood baseball games when you're eliminated in the varsity tryouts? What do you say to your folks when your SAT scores are too low for you to get into the college of your choice?"

From these questions, you will be able to determine the focus this session on failure should have for your group. Ask the planning group to look at each activity and decide whether or not it will work with your group and whether or not it will help you achieve your revised goal. This plan suggests using graffiti. Will the group take the graffiti seriously? If not, what can you substitute for this? What about the discussion questions? You may need to write some possible questions out in advance. The Bible study is done in small groups. This is the heart of the session, where they discover how Jesus handled failure. Do you think the small groups will be able to function without leadership? Should one member of the planning committee be assigned to work with each group? What do you think the groups should discover? Try studying the passage yourself and writing out your discoveries.

After the session is over, you will want to evaluate with the planning group what happened in the session. Were you accurate in your understanding of where youth were in dealing with failure? Do you think the session helped them get any new insights into this? Do you think they can handle failure better now? Which activities worked? Which activities fell flat? What does this tell you about your next session?

SOME EARLY PITFALLS IN YOUTH LEADERSHIP

There is no guarantee that just because you have developed skill in relating with youth, teaching, and planning, your first or even second and third meetings with your group will go smoothly. Any number of things could happen which you cannot foresee. For example:

What If . . .

● *You ask students in your first session to make name tags and they balk, saying, "We did that in kindergarten."* You can say, "I understand how you feel, but I need to get to know you. Can you think of another way of doing this?"

● *Fifteen youth attended your first session. You arrive for the second session and only three youth are there.* If it is possible to use your session plan with only three persons, go ahead. If not, suggest that you go out for a Coke and spend the hour getting better acquainted. During the week, call the students who were not there and find out what you can do, together, to prevent this kind of thing from happening again.

● *One person in your group continually interrupts you, makes wisecracks, and engages in a lot of disruptive horseplay.* You will learn later of creative ways of dealing with discipline problems. At this stage of the game, however, you could simply tell the person that you are having a difficult time getting through the new experience of teaching and this person is making it even more difficult. Invite her or him either to leave or cooperate with you. (If another person is working with you, this person may spend the session time with the disruptive person away from the group.)

● *The group is apathetic. They go through the motions of doing what you suggest, but don't seem excited.* You may have to put up with this apathy for awhile. Later, when you know them better, you may understand the cause of their apathy and come up with some things, together, which will turn the group on.

● *There are cliques that always do things together, making others feel left out.* You should assign people to small groups—don't let them select their own groups. Keep people moving from group to group as much as possible. Do not do too many total group activities which will provide an opportunity for cliques to form.

● *The group keeps talking about the leader they had last year.* You will have to listen to this for awhile, rejoicing with the group that they had such a great experience. But don't try to copy what the former leader did. You are a different person. Be confident in your own abilities. In time, they will come to appreciate you for yourself and will not make comparisons with the past.

SUMMARY

The last three chapters have presented some basic skills for surviving the first few weeks of an experience as a youth leader: becoming-acquainted skills, teaching skills, and planning skills. These chapters have intentionally given very elementary information. We have assumed that a new leader needs first to work within a very structured situation, using skills which are easily mastered. Once you feel comfortable in this type of situation, you will have the confidence to move out into more creative leadership.

The important thing is not to remain at the level of structured leadership. It's a comfortable spot to be in. You can quickly master the skills required, and you are soon operating automatically, finding that it takes less and less time to prepare a session and come up with a smooth learning experience. The problem is that it can become so mechanical that it is boring and little real learning is taking place. You need to move on to the more creative level where you are able to respond spontaneously as needs arise. The next chapters will help in this transition.

Section 2
Understanding
Youth

Myths About Youth 4

All of us approach a new group of people with some apprehension. What will they be like? Will we be accepted? Will they like us? Will we like them? When we approach a new group of youth, our apprehension sometimes is greater than when we join a group of people our own age. In many ways, we feel like foreigners approaching a strange country. We don't know the language (It changes from year to year!). We wear a different style of clothes. Our ideas seem out-of-date.

Our feelings are very much like those of youth themselves in the presence of adults. We feel awkward. How can we overcome this? How can we break down the barriers and feel not only comfortable but also accepted, liked, and at home with a group of youth? How can we move from feeling "at home" to becoming effective youth leaders?

DEBUNKING THE MYTHS

To begin with, we need to look realistically at some of the myths about youth and their world which lead to misunderstandings and shallow relationships between adults and youth. The following are samples of these myths. You will be able to add more from your own experience.

(We are defining myths here as statements which have some basis in fact but which are exaggerated generalizations.)

All youth are alike; if you know one, you know them all.

This is one of the most dangerous myths about youth. First of all, it is untrue. How many of us feel that knowing one man or woman automatically assures that we understand everyone.

Second, it is dehumanizing. It makes us treat youth not as persons but as an age-group. It is important to know the various

33

developmental stages youth may be going through (and we'll get to that later in this chapter). However, the youth "expert" who can describe adolescence as a psychological stage, but who cannot carry on a conversation with sixteen-year-old Jim is of little value as a youth leader. Similarly, the youth "expert" who tries to fit Jim and Rosalyn and Art into the "normal" pattern for youth is also dangerous. The normal pattern is based on observations of many Jims and Rosalyns and Arts. It is the average of the behavior of many people, and there are nearly as many persons on both ends of the scale above and below this average as there are in the middle. This will become a little more clear as we talk about youth age-group characteristics later; for now it is important to think of each young person as unique, with special skills, a personality like no one else's, and gifts to offer us and our group.

Youth resent adults; they would rather spend their time with other youth than with adults.

It is true that youth like to spend time with their peers. To a great extent, this has been encouraged by our society, which segregates them in schools, clubs, and employment opportunities. But most youth we know would like to spend some of their time with an adult who understands them, listens to them, and offers a significant relationship.

Think back to your own adolescence. Didn't you have a favorite adult whom you sought out when you had problems or when you had good news or just to be with? Most youth need this as they make the transition into the adult world.

Most adults are afraid of youth.

Many adults are afraid to try relating with youth. They feel alien to the youth culture. They feel youth will laugh at them or think them "square" or just ignore them. Many adults, however, have developed meaningful relationships with youth and consider some youth to be very good friends. They enjoy being with them, learning from them, seeing life from their perspective, and gaining insights from their culture.

Youth are self-centered; they don't care about anyone but themselves.

Some youth, in fact many youth, are caught up in a search for personal meaning that makes them spend great amounts of time in introspective soul-searching. However, most youth we know are also very much aware of other people. They respond willingly to bike-a-thons for hunger campaigns, filling sandbags for flood protection, and work projects in their neighborhoods. It is true that they often find it easier to respond to impersonal helping activities than to needs of their peers, but this latter kind of involvement comes with maturity and with a secure self-image, which many youth are in the process of forming.

Youth don't really like serious discussions.

If you have giggling teenagers around your house or if you ride public transportation during school commuting hours, you might be tempted to believe this myth. But anyone who has attended a youth conference or taken a group of youth on a weekend retreat will have to disown it. Those all-night bull sessions eventually turn to very serious topics: What is love? Is there life after death? Can you believe everything in the Bible?

At one youth conference in which I served on the leadership team, I found myself constantly irritated by two boys who always arrived late at our small group and never entered into group activities because they were so groggy from such bull sessions. When I talked with them in the middle of the week, I discovered that their all-night vigils had been devoted to extremely serious questions and that they had probably been getting more from these conversations than they could ever have gotten from our small group. This is not to overlook the effect on the group of their nonparticipation, with which we had to deal, but simply to illustrate that youth probably engage in serious discussions more often than most adults. They are facing serious decisions, and they need time to talk with their peers—and with adults—about their options.

Youth don't follow through on responsibilities.

Some youth who are assigned to church boards or committees or who are asked to take responsibilites for youth group programs will not carry out these assignments. But some *adults* are also known to have failed to carry out their responsibilities. Again, individuals are different. Youth who have learned at home or in school to handle responsibility can be trusted to follow through; other youth will let you and the group down. Youth on church boards and committees need training in the way committees operate and adults who enable them to make meaningful contributions.

Our society does not permit youth to take much serious responsibility. As youth leaders, we can help youth by giving them increasing amounts or responsibility and supporting them as they learn to handle it.

If you get boys to attend your youth group or class, the girls will follow.

In these days of liberation, a statement like the above might seem chauvinistic, but it's still being heard. It is true that youth like a place where they can meet members of the opposite sex, and the church often provides this place. But our experience has been that neither sex has more drawing power than the other. This may not be an acceptable motive for building up a group, unless the purpose of the group is getting the sexes together!

All youth are rebellious.

This is a tricky statement. Most youth go through a period of experimentation with behavior, values, and ideas. They form their own behavior patterns, and these often differ from those of significant adults in their lives. However, the difference is a matter of degree. Most adolescent psychologists agree that high school youth are more likely to be like their parents in their behavior and their ideas than they are to be unlike them. Most youth do not really pull away and form different life-styles until they reach college or the working world because only then do they have the financial and emotional independence to do this.

But the word "rebellious" is key in this myth. This word is defined in different ways by different people. It covers a whole range of behavior from playing rock music at eardrum-piercing levels to smoking pot. "Rebellious" should be a term that is reserved for youth who consistently behave in ways which are either illegal or at least highly disturbing to others and who continue in this behavior in order to (a) disturb others purposely, (b) harm themselves, or (c) express preference for a special peer group's values over those of significant adults.

For example, the youth who has to be told, not once but many times, to turn down the stereo when you are watching TV might be considered rebellious, as would the youth who collects speeding tickets or comes home stoned every Saturday night. The youth who is constantly negative is rebellious in a passive way.

Youth who are consistently rebellious are the exception rather than the rule. And their behavior generally has roots in problems that began before adolescence or problems in the community at large, such as an unsupportive or inconsistent home environment, unusual competition between siblings, a school system which rewards only top academic achievers, a community without adequate youth recreational opportunities. If most of the youth you know tend to be rebellious when rebellion is defined as consistently deviant behavior, perhaps you should take a close look at the reasons for this.

Today's youth are more sophisticated, more knowledgeable, more experienced than ever before.

Like most myths, there is a grain of truth in this statement. There are *some* youth who fit the above description. Television has made it possible for more youth than ever before to be exposed to world events, political discussions, and cultural happenings. Inexpensive transportation and special youth fares have made it possible for more youth to travel both in the United States and abroad. Urbanization has brought increased opportunities for social interaction.

However, we must beware, once again, of applying generalizations to all youth. In traveling around the country, I have seen youth who are very sophisticated and knowledgeable and youth who are not. The section of the country in which a person lives does not seem to be a factor in this, nor does, necessarily, the size of the community or economic level of the family. Some very affluent youth have no direct knowledge of racial problems in this country, and some rural youth have spent the summer in Europe. It is important for us to become aware of where youth are in our own community and not apply generalizations.

Youth aren't interested in religion.

The media have recently been attempting to break down this myth emphasizing the religious cults in America which are appealing especially to the young. This leads to the reverse myth that all youth *are* interested in religion. Neither statement is completely true. It is safe to say that some time during adolescence youth will raise questions about God, the Bible, a personal faith, and an ethical standard for behavior. Some youth will become quite wrapped up in these questions and may experiment with various types of solutions—try out different churches, different sects, different patterns of behavior. Other youth will attend church regularly and discuss the questions as opportunities become available and as they become involved in relationships of trust with persons who can deal with these questions. Other youth will be on the fringe of the church or will turn off institutional religion altogether. In this area, as in other areas in which generalizations are made, youth respond as individuals.

In your own group, you may have some youth who never discuss religious topics, but remain with your church-affiliated group because it meets some social or personal needs (which, in themselves, could be called "religious") and other youth who will become involved in a search for personal religious meaning.

Most adults don't really enjoy being with youth.

Many adults initially feel uncomfortable with youth, especially with a group of youth. However, once steps have been taken to overcome these feelings and to develop genuine relationships with individual youth, many adults find themselves really looking forward to being with youth.

A personal experience might illustrate this. I found myself attending several youth conferences within the past year after two years of very minimal contact with youth. When I walked into the first conference, a feeling of excitement surged through me. Everyone seemed so alive! There was music and horseplay and serious questioning. I enjoyed being there. And I think most adults who have had significant experiences with youth feel the same way. It's fun!

SUMMARY

The myths which have been exposed in this chapter represent only a small number of the misconceptions people have about youth. But they point out the danger that exists when we make broad generalizations based on limited experience. There is a grain of truth in each statement, but believing it in entirety can distort our understanding of youth as an age group and impair our relationships with individual youth.

Try writing down any broad statements you have heard about youth which are not given above. Examine these statements closely. Are they really true or are they myths?

It's important to move beyond misinformation about youth to a deeper understanding of how youth as an age group are really different from adults and children and to make generalizations based on sound research rather than on popular media reports.

Common Characteristics of Youth | 5

Once we have disposed of some of the myths that block our relationships with youth, we are free to look at some accurate statements about youth as an age-group to see what characteristics youth tend to have in common. In doing this, however, we need to raise the caution which was implied in several of the debunked myths:

Don't expect all youth to act alike. They're individuals!

One of the greatest risks we take in even mentioning characteristics youth have in common is that we will look at Dave and expect him to fit into a preconceived pattern of behavior, thinking he is abnormal if he doesn't. Or we will dismiss some real needs of Marcia by saying, "It's just a stage she's going through; she'll grow out of it."

As we consider the following generalizations about youth, think of each characteristic as being a telephone line with six crows huddled together in the middle and three on each of the extreme ends. The crows in the middle represent most youth in relation to a particular characteristic, but some youth (the crows at the extreme ends) will exhibit this characteristic either minimally or more than the average. For example, the majority of adolescents may reach sexual maturation at fourteen, but some will be way ahead of the others and some way behind.

Then think of a series of telephone lines, one for each characteristic. Crows from the middle of the first line fly to the end of the next line and crows from the end of the first line fly to the middle of the second line. This describes the way in which youth vary from one characteristic to another. They may be "normal" in one area, but ahead or behind the majority of their peers in another. (They may mature sexually at the average age, but be behind their peers in emotional maturity.)

With these cautions in mind, let's take the plunge and see what youth have in common and how we can relate to them better through a knowledge of these common characteristics.

PHYSICAL DEVELOPMENT

Historically, the beginning of adolescence has been defined in strictly physical terms as the onset of puberty. It is the time when boys discover that first facial fuzz and girls find their chests are no longer flat. It is the beginning of sexual maturation.

Accompanying this sudden surge of hormones is bodily growth which is sometimes sporadic, leading to physical awkwardness, huge consumption of food, a lack of energy, and an increased need for long periods of sleep or, on the other hand, sudden bursts of energy. There is a new consciousness of physical strength.

As the adolescent matures, there is increased control over the body. There is a consciousness of physical potential and pride in accomplishments involving skill such as mechanics, sewing, sports, dancing, cooking, or driving.

Different rates of physical growth and sexual maturation are of great concern to most youth. The girl who is still flat-chested at sixteen and the boy who hasn't used a razor at seventeen suffer untold embarrassment. Similarly, the boy who doesn't shoot up to six feet or the girl who does is intensely self-conscious in the presence of his or her more "normal" peers. The too-fat teen or the too-skinny teen, the youth with a long nose, buck teeth, or acne, all suffer varying degrees of self-debasement.

Think back to your own adolescence. What was there about your physical appearance that embarrassed you? Do you find it "silly" now? It wasn't then. It was something you worried about each time you looked in the mirror. It may even have kept you from going to parties, wearing certain styles of clothing, or playing a sport in which you were really interested.

As youth leaders, we need to be very much aware of the concern youth in our group feel about their physical appearance. We need to provide opportunities for them to talk about this concern and discover that they are not alone in feeling the way they do. We need to help them be realistic. A boy who is overweight should be concerned enough to go on a diet, but he should not have to feel that he is unlovable because of his size.

We should be very careful about the kinds of physical activities we encourage in our youth program. Individual or team competition, for example, emphasizes physical differences, while group activities help members compensate for each other's weaknesses and strengths. Rather than organizing a basketball team, you might put your group through a survival training course in which each person helps the other master skills.

There should be many opportunities for affirmation. Especially in the church, youth should find that physical strengths and weaknesses are not the criteria for acceptance. They should feel they are accepted because they are unique individuals who are loved for themselves—not for what they can do.

Opportunities should also be provided for dealing with the concern—and even anxiety—youth feel about their sexuality. Teens are faced with an extremely serious dilemma in this area. They are not able to achieve financial independence, and thus handle the responsibility of a family, until they are in their late teens or early twenties. However, they reach sexual maturation in their midteens. They are biologically ready for sexual experience, but it must be postponed.

As adults, we often forget the strain this dilemma creates for teens. Any experimentation with their new sexual urges must be within narrow limits. If they exceed these limits, as so easily happens in the heat of an emotional involvement, they experience strong guilt feelings as well as, in some cases, serious consequences.

Some teens, who feel they are unable to wait, enter into an early marriage. But this is seldom an adequate solution, as the number of divorces in such marriages indicates. "The pill," or other contraceptives, has been another solution, but these carry their own load of guilt as well as some possible medical consequences. And, of course, abortion or adoption are controversial last resorts when pregnancy occurs.

It is impossible for us to suggest simple solutions in the area of sexual behavior. This would take a book in itself. But we can give some guidelines through which you can find your own answers. You can create an atmosphere of openness and acceptance in your group so questions about sexual behavior can be raised. Know where you stand on the subject and how the parents of the youth feel. Do not oversimplify the problem; there are no easy answers and no one solution for everyone. Invite trained resource persons to your group to help youth deal with alternative types of behavior: doctors, social workers, persons from the Planned Parenthood Association, your minister. Be informed and open and you'll find ways to help your group find its own answers.

MENTAL DEVELOPMENT

Most of us realize that it is easier to carry on an intelligent conversation or to reason with adolescents than it is with younger children. For one thing, they are beginning to speak "our" language. Their vocabulary is similar to the one we use. We don't have to simplify the "big words" we use in our ordinary conversation.

But increased vocabulary is just one aspect of the mental development of adolescents. They are also maturing in their mental processes. They are no longer bound to concrete thinking, but are beginning to think abstractly. They do not have to see a rocket orbited into space to understand how it might work or experience discrimination to understand what prejudice is all about.

The ability to think abstractly is an extremely important characteristic in terms of religious teaching. It is the reason many churches accept teenagers rather than young children into full membership. Faith is basically an abstract concept. It is difficult for young children to understand what faith is, what it means to believe in and respond to God's love. Teenagers, however, can begin to understand and deal with these faith concepts.

Adolescents are also able to think more scientifically and objectively. They are able to develop hypotheses and test them against evidence to come up with a solution. They can deal with several alternative solutions to the problem of using the family car, whereas younger children would tend to see only one answer.

In terms of religious education, the ability to think scientifically and objectively is again a "plus." As youth study the Bible, they can begin to accept it as a book of faith with many interpretations and can determine which interpretations fit best with their own experience. In the same way, they can discuss social problems and come up with a number of possible solutions.

The intellectual processes of youth are much more introspective, analytical, and even self-critical than those of children. They spend a great deal of time trying to "find out who they are." They write poetry which is very subjective. They spend hours trying out new ideas on their friends. As youth leaders, we can provide opportunities for this kind of discussion in informal meetings where youth feel free to share their most personal thoughts. We can challenge their ideas, in an accepting way, and help them refine their mental processes.

Youth are also able to think realistically about the future. They can project what might happen and are, of course, very concerned about their own futures. We have an opportunity, as youth leaders, to help them become intentional in planning their futures, to consider all of their options, and to make decisions with which they will be able to live.

Because youth are maturing mentally at different rates (just as they mature physically at different rates), we need to provide a wide selection of learning activities for them. Discussion, research, debates, projects, creative expression, drama, and role play are all activities which should be considered. We should *never* get into the rut of relying only on lecture and discussion. This is a dull technique even for adults, and it will not work with some youth who have not yet achieved the height of their abstract reasoning powers.

EMOTIONAL DEVELOPMENT

Adolescence seems to both youth and adults to be a time of tremendous emotional upheaval. Adults talk about youth being moody, sullen, silly, argumentative, and flighty. Youth describe themselves as on a high one moment and down in the depths another. They seem to feel every emotion more keenly than ever. They are madly in love, seething with anger, bored to death.

Part of this emotional upheaval is based on real physical changes which are taking place within adolescents. As they mature physically, their hormone balance changes and their emotions are directly affected.

Another part of the picture is their increased intellectual awareness of their emotions. As they begin to be able to think subjectively and abstractly, they are able to separate out their emotions, put labels on them, and describe them—often in exaggerated terms.

Still another factor is the lack of experience of adolescents in handling new emotions. When youth fall in love for the first time or respond with ecstasy to a new piece of music or are filled with rage, it is frightening. They are not sure where their emotions will take them—whether they will be able to control them. Often, at first, they do lose control. It takes experience to reach the fine balance between expressing our emotions authentically while behaving rationally and within the bounds of social control. Teens are just beginning to experiment with this, and they inevitably move too far in one direction or the other at first.

As youth leaders, we need to be aware that adolescence *is* a time of tremendous emotional upheaval. We need to accept this fact and not be surprised or overly concerned when youth swing from one emotion to another. At the same time, we need to help them understand what they are going through, to help them accept their own emotions as real and good, and to provide situations in which they can experiment with expressing their emotions without hurting themselves or others. A warm, accepting group is the best place for youth to learn to handle their new emotions. Adults who are not personally threatened by angry verbal attacks or occasional apathy can help youth move from extreme emotional outbursts to a balanced control.

At the same time, we need, as youth leaders, to be alert for signs that some youth might be in serious emotional difficulty. While occasional swings in mood are normal in adolescence, extreme and frequent swings might signal emotional problems which could become serious. Similarly, occasional withdrawal, quietness, or crying spells are normal, but if such behavior continues for a long time, it could be a sign of a serious depression. If you are concerned about such behavior in your group, seek the advice of a professional counselor to determine whether there is a situation which should receive professional attention.

SOCIAL DEVELOPMENT

Adolescence is a time when social development takes several leaps forward. While relationships within the home are primary for the young child and later for the adult, peer relationships are of utmost importance for adolescents.

Most youth begin their teenage social development with a close, exclusive relationship with one or two "best friends." The key word here is exclusive. While youth continue to have "best friends" into their adult years, they spend most of their time with one or two other people in early adolescence and develop a very dependent relationship with them.

This is natural when we understand what is happening in other areas of the adolescent's life. This is a time when new emotions are surfacing, new ideas are being explored, new behavior is examined. It is a time of change. This change can take place best in the context of a close, noncritical relationship. The youth will not have to suffer others' laughter, ridicule, and rejection because there is a "best friend" who will accept his or her behavior regardless of how "out of character" it may be.

When early adolescents do relate to larger groups of people or to a "gang," it is a very impersonal kind of relationship. They do not share much of their real selves and often play a role which is quite unlike their behavior with their close friends.

As adolescents mature, they begin to become more secure and confident about "who they are." They move more comfortably into a variety of relationships with a variety of people, including adults, younger children, and peers with whom they have had no relationship before.

To facilitate this movement, we, as youth leaders, need to provide a group atmosphere in which youth can be themselves—whoever that self may be at the moment—without risk of rejection. We must allow for a variety of relationships to develop. There should be times when very good friends can do things together and other times when youth can relate to the group as a whole. We should try to help youth develop confidence in themselves and move away from dependence on the approval of one or two other people. We should try, above all, to keep our group from becoming a clique or from developing cliques within it because cliques inevitably limit other relationships and social growth.

One other aspect of social development needs to be discussed. As adolescents begin to explore who they are in relationship to their peers, they experiment with various kinds of social behavior. They follow the examples of the "trend setters" in their group by experimenting with smoking, alcohol, drugs, sex, language, and even vandalism.

Peer pressure is a very real problem, especially for persons who enter adolescence with low self-images. You, as an adult leader, may be able to counteract negative peer pressure by providing a group in which the standards are positive: persons are accepted for who they are and not forced to play roles; persons are encouraged to express their individuality; they are provided with creative outlets for their energy; there is opportunity to discuss the consequences of such behavior as smoking and the use of drugs and alcohol. This kind of group and how you develop it is discussed in detail in the next chapter.

MORAL DEVELOPMENT

In church education we often make the mistake of assuming that a moral code must be taught only to young children and that once it has been taught, it will determine the behavior of the person for a lifetime. However, persons mature in their moral judgment just as in other areas of their lives. A child accepts certain behavior as "right" or "wrong" because the persons who are in authority (parents, teachers, ministers) say it is right or wrong. Adolescents begin to question the authority of these persons and to develop their own moral viewpoint.

Youth recognize that there are a number of moral standards and that these standards change. They begin to explore the standards that they can accept for their own behavior. As pointed out in the last section, their peer group plays a large role in their choice of moral standards. However, parents and childhood experiences are also important.

Adolescents begin to accept the fact that moral standards can be different for different people. They feel that what is right for them is not necessarily right for everyone else. They do not condemn their friends for smoking, even though they decide this is not something they want to do.

They also begin to look for broad principles which determine whether behavior is right or wrong. Stealing is not only wrong because there are laws which condemn it but also because the welfare of all would be threatened if stealing were tolerated.

They begin to be concerned about justice for others, in comparison with their earlier childhood concern with justice only for themselves.

Adolescents experience a lot of anxiety as they deal with moral decisions. Life is no longer a simple path of right and wrong. They are faced with many moral standards, a questioning of authority, a concern with justice for other persons. Each new moral decision demands a new round of questions, critiques, and experimentation.

The church can help adolescents in their search for moral standards by providing a nonjudgmental atmosphere in which they can explore various alternatives. Of course, the church has its own set of moral standards which it hopes youth will accept, but these cannot be forced on adolescents. They must examine them along with others and reach their own conclusions. This is difficult for some adults to facilitate. It is easier to be dogmatic, simply to tell youth that the church teaches us to act in a certain way and that this should be accepted without question. However, most youth will reject this kind of stance and will probably be turned away from the church rather than come around to its point of view.

We will do better simply to present the church's view as one which we accept and live by, and let youth explore it as one alternative. Most church-oriented youth will eventually accept the church's standards when they are free to make their own choice.

Perhaps we should add that moral standards are often accepted through identification with significant adults. If we develop meaningful relationships with youth in our group, they will be more likely to be attracted to the standards by which we live.

SUMMARY

The one thing which we hope comes through above everything else in this chapter is that we must get to know youth as individuals and not look at them simply as an age group.

However, we can make some generalizations about the developmental characteristics of adolescents which can enable us to relate to them at the level of their deepest concerns and "bridge the gap" between our adult world and their youth world. The following chart illustrates this:

Because youth are . . .	We should . . .
Concerned about varying rates of physical development and physical abnormalities . . .	Be sensitive to their concern for physical problems, help youth be realistic about such problems, provide opportunities for dealing with this concern with affirmation.
Biologically ready for sexual experience, but unable to handle a responsible marriage . . .	Provide a group which is open to questions about sexual behavior, provide resources which will help youth deal with alternatives in behavior, share our own standards.
Moving from concrete thinking to abstract thinking, able to think scientifically and introspectively, able to project their thoughts into the future . . .	Provide problem-solving learning experiences, allow for many informal discussions, accept questions and doubts about the faith, help youth find their own answers.

Because youth are . . .

We should . . .

Developing mentally at different rates . . .

Provide a wide selection of learning activities.

Experiencing emotional upheaval due to hormonal changes and inexperience in handling new emotions . . .

Accept a wide range of emotional expression without criticism, avoid becoming personally threatened by angry verbal attacks or occasional apathy, provide an accepting group where youth can experiment with emotional expression, be alert for emotional problems.

Moving from dependent relationships with "best friends" to a variety of relationships with a variety of people . . .

Provide for a variety of relationships—times when best friends can relate and times when youth must relate to the group, discourage cliques.

Experimenting with social behavior and following the example of "trend setters" among their peers . . .

Encourage youth to have confidence in their own standards, provide a group which has positive social behavior standards, help youth face the possible consequences of their behavior.

Exploring a number of moral standards and selecting ones they can affirm . . .

Provide a nonjudgmental atmosphere where a variety of moral standards can be explored, but be clear about our own standards and those of the church, develop significant personal relationships with youth who may then identify with our standards.

Concerned about justice for others . . .

Provide opportunities for involvement in social change which results in justice.

Understanding the ways in which youth develop through adolescence should help us, as leaders, both relate better to them and facilitate their development.

It should help us see our role not as that of a parent ("You should behave in this way.") or as an older sibling ("I was where you are only a few years ago.") or as an adult who is still a youth at heart ("Bring in the pot and I'll smoke it with you."), but as an authentic adult with whom youth can test their own behavior and ideas. We must be warm and accepting of the problems youth are facing and helpful as well in facilitating their solutions to these problems. We must be sure of our own faith so we can communicate it, not dogmatically, but in the context of a caring relationship.

Finally, understanding where youth are should help us see the need for establishing a group which is nonjudgmental, accepting, and open—a group in which youth can express their anxieties, ask questions, try new behavior without risking rejection or harming themselves or others. This kind of group—and how it is developed—will be discussed in more detail in the next section.

Section 3
Beyond Survival:
Skills for the
Experienced Leader

Planning Group Experiences 6

As we become better acquainted with members of our group and come to know them as individuals, we realize that if we are to respond to their needs, we cannot always rely on the material available in packaged programs. We find that a study of the good Samaritan is interesting to Al, who came into the group from a nonchurch background, but it's old hat to Rebecca, who studied it in the sixth grade. We come into the group on Sunday night and find everyone talking about a tragic accident which killed a fellow classmate and realize we can't use the program on world mission we had scheduled. We learn that Art is staying away from the group because he feels others don't like him; our preoccupation with the session plan has made us unaware of his problems.

We also discover that following a structured design week after week without any alteration can be repetitious and even boring—both for the members of the group and for us as leaders. No one feels excited about the group meeting. Attendance may even begin to drop as members express nonverbally that things have gotten predictable and dull.

These are clues that it's time to move from our safe, comfortable spot of "following the book" to a style of leadership which allows us to respond spontaneously to individual needs and creatively to adapt resource materials to fit our group. We've come to the point that a good cook comes to when he realizes a few more eggs or a dash of oregano would improve a recipe, or when a seamstress discovers that the sleeves from one pattern will enhance a dress of a different pattern. We are ready to adapt, create, improvise—to break out on our own into creative leadership.

Knowing the time for this is ripe, how do we make the big plunge? How do we get up the nerve to experiment, to risk making mistakes, to dare to move beyond mere survival to situations which promote greater growth?

Part of the answer is experience. As we develop confidence in our abilities and skill, we can release our own creativity and that of our group. We can feel free to change session plans and sometimes even create new ones because we are comfortable with the basic skills of leadership.

Another part of the answer is knowing enough about the components of group leadership that we are able to respond to needs as they arise—just as the cook mentioned earlier knows enough about cooking ingredients to know which spice to use to achieve the particular taste desired. This section will help you become familiar with these components: planning skills, group process, the leader's role, teaching methods for the experienced leader, and choosing resources.

Finally, it is necessary to be very aware of our objectives—to pinpoint just what "taste" we are looking for, to identify what we mean by learning situations which promote real growth.

WHAT WE'RE ABOUT

In church education, our objective has been defined in various ways at various times as "the new person in Jesus Christ," "knowing the living God," etc. I like to define our objective as helping persons experience the gospel. This means that, as church educators, we are not only helping persons to know the Good News but we are also helping them actually to live the abundant life. It means we are providing experiences in which persons can make life decisions based on their Christian faith; situations in which they can embrace values which affirm the Christian principles of personal worth, concern for others, and a vital relationship with God; and situations in which they can become actively involved in mission in their own church, community, and throughout the world.

In short, we need to provide situations in which persons can find meaning in the gospel and can apply this meaning to their own lives. We need to provide experiences, not just lectures.

PLANNING LEARNING EXPERIENCES

How do we know what learning experiences to plan? How can we determine what situations will promote real growth—when it is defined as finding meaning in the gospel and applying this meaning to daily life situations?

We mentioned in the first chapter that, as inexperienced youth leaders, we should insist that our church provide us with educationally sound resources which are based on curriculum writers' research into the best kinds of learning experiences for our age group. As we become more experienced, however, we discover that the effective use of these resources requires us to adapt them to meet the needs that emerge in our own group. This may even involve mixing learning experiences from several resources. Not everyone is ready to study the same thing at the same time, as we pointed out at the beginning of this chapter. And real learning will not take place unless some degree of readiness is present—unless members of the group have an interest in learning the subject which is presented, unless it meets a real need.

I can teach the origins of the Bible to a group of tenth graders (as I once attempted to do), and they will tune me out unless they have a genuine interest in how the Bible came to be written or unless I can show some real connection between such a study and a present concern of theirs, such as whether or not to cheat on exams.

All of this implies that we need to be very aware of where our group members are—what kinds of growth they need and are ready to develop.

To some extent, it is impossible to know this for each individual in the group, or at least to respond to each level of need for each individual. To do this, we would have to have a one-to-one relationship with each member of the group all of the time. The best we can do is to "prioritize" the needs of the group and respond to those which seem to be most universal and most urgent. This gets us into a planning process.

Planning on the Basis of Needs

The following process can be used for planning one class session (compare it with the session plan on pages 26 and 27), for planning a series of meetings, for planning a retreat, a worship service, or a bowling party. It is simply a design for planning. We will describe its use in planning a learning experience.

Step One: Gather Data

This is the step we began discussing above—finding out what needs exist in the group, what subject the majority are most ready to explore.

We can collect data in several ways. One way is to brainstorm.

Ask the group to throw out ideas for discussion topics. List them all, clarify any which need clarifying, and then vote on the subject the group wants most to explore. (See the description of brainstorming on pages 17 and 18.)

Another method is to use a questionnaire dealing with problems youth are facing. From your own observation of the group, develop a questionnaire which lists problem areas. (A sample questionnaire is given in the Appendix, pages 118 and 119.) Have students rate the problems about which they have the most concern. Develop a unit based on the problems which appear most often.

Still another method is to determine subjects about which youth feel strongly—either negatively or positively, but strongly. Make a list of controversial topics, perhaps ones which are covered in your resource material. For example, one resource has sessions on the following: privacy, death, politics, reading the Bible, parents, intergenerational worship, ecology, leisure, running away. Write out statements about these topics and have youth mark whether they feel strongly about them by placing a key word from the statement on a ladder. A sample of this technique is given in the Appendix, page 120.

Another method for determining the needs in your group is simply observing the members' behavior. In the example we gave at the beginning of this chapter, we suggested that the group might be faced with a crisis—the death of a friend—or with a situation in which one member feels the others don't like him or her. In the first situation, you will know that the group needs to deal with the subject of death and in the second, with how to make members feel welcome in the group.

A final method of getting at concerns of the group is to have them respond to open-ended statements like the following:

When I am alone, I wonder about . . .
The thing I worry about most is . . .
I become really angry when . . .
The worst thing that could happen to me is . . .
I am afraid that . . .

This type of question gets at some feelings which push youth to a deeper level of sharing concerns.

Once you have chosen a general subject area, write out specific statements that describe the problems in this area. For example, let's assume that you have discovered the following from a questionnaire administered to the group:

- Most of the group marked problems with parents as their area of greatest concern.
- Several group members live with only one parent.
- One group member recently ran away because she couldn't handle her problems with her parents.
- Most problems with parents center upon communication ("My parents don't listen to me."), values ("My parents don't think I should hang around with kids who drink."), expectations ("My parents are always pushing me to do better in school or try out for the basketball team or something."), rules ("My parents want me in by ten o'clock, even on weekends."), and caring ("My parents don't seem to notice if I'm around; they're too wrapped up in their own friends and jobs to care.").
- Some group members seem to have few problems with their parents.

Step Two: Data Analysis

Once you have gathered all of your data, you will need to look at it carefully to see what it means. You will need to identify the major problems and decide which are the most serious or which are problems for the majority of the group.

In the example above, it is evident that an important subject area is problems with parents. But there are many kinds of problems: communication, value conflicts, expectations, rules, caring. Which problems seem to crop up most often for most of the group members? These are the problems to focus on in your unit.

Several group members live with only one parent. You will have to keep this in mind as you design your study and perhaps provide special resources for these persons.

What about the girl who ran away? Has she worked through her own feelings well enough to take part in a rational discussion of problems with parents or is the subject still too emotionally loaded for her? What about the group members who do not have major problems with their parents? Can they find ways to fit into the discussion?

Step Three: Write the Objective

Be realistic here. You cannot solve all problems. What can you do in the time and with the resources you have available?

Your objective should be achievable; that is, you should be able to accomplish it. And it should be measurable; you should be able to tell to what degree you have achieved it. It should be a state-

ment of results, not of how you are going to go about your study.
How will members of your group change, grow, or act differently
as a result of this study?

The objective should be specific, not general. What specific
things do you want to see changed?

Using the example above, let's assume that your data analysis
has led you to believe that parents and youth are not communicating. From your own knowledge of communication, you know that
listening is one of the most important skills in communication.
You decide that the group should develop skill in listening. A
possible objective for your unit might be: Youth will be able to
label their problems with listening to their parents and will increase their skill in listening.

Step Four: Develop Strategy

The strategy we're talking about here is the same as
coaches use on the football field—ways of reaching our objective.

If you want to have members of your group develop skill in
labeling their problems with listening, you will have to spend time
talking about these problems and discriminating between them.
This means having role plays or discussions or simulation games
in which the problems are brought into the open and labels can be
put on them. Then, if you want to help the group develop skill in
listening, you will need to provide opportunities for them to
practice listening and evaluation of their improvement in mastering this skill.

When you are more experienced in leadership, you will be able
to develop learning activities yourself to meet your objectives (see
chapters 9 and 10). At this point, however, it would be best to find
the problem area and use the learning activities suggested in
various resources. For example, in order to meet the objective on
listening skills, look for resources on communication with sessions
on listening skills.

Step Five: Evaluation

If you have developed a clear objective, your evaluation
should be easy. You will simply need to test whether your objective has been met.

Evaluation can be done in several ways. You can use short-
answer, sentence completion, contrasting statement, or
multiple-choice questionnaires. You can talk informally with
group members to see how they feel they have improved. You can

use rating or ranking scales. (Examples of these methods can be found in the Appendix, pages 118 to 120.)

To evaluate the objective we gave above ("Youth will be able to label their problems with listening to their parents and will increase their skill in listening."), you might have a session in which you read some hypothetical case studies of communication problems with parents and ask members of the group to label the problems and identify ways the behavior might change.

One thing you should avoid in evaluation is questions which are too general. For example, you should not ask, "How did you like this unit?" People will say, "It was okay" or "Ugh" or "It was the best unit we ever had." This doesn't tell you what was right or wrong, or what was learned. Evaluation which is not based on your objective is not helpful evaluation.

SUMMARY

Before beginning to plan with your group, it is important to have in mind what you are trying to do in youth ministry. The overall objective for youth ministry can be stated as helping persons experience the gospel; that is, providing experiences in which they can make life decisions based on their Christian faith; situations in which they embrace values which affirm the Christian principles of personal worth, concern for others, and a vital relationship with God and situations in which they can become actively involved in mission in their own church, community, and throughout the world.

When planning specific experiences for the group, the planning process outlined in this chapter should be used in order to insure that you are meeting real needs. This process consists of five steps: gathering data, analyzing data, writing an objective, developing strategy, and evaluating the results.

This planning process can be used for any kind of planning, from planning which unit to study in a church school class to planning a weekend retreat.

In conclusion, we should raise a caution. Many leaders begin with strategies. They pick up a resource book, find a session which looks interesting, and present it without knowing whether it meets any needs or without having any clear objective in mind. Try to discipline yourself to begin with data collection. That's the only way really to meet the needs of your group.

The correct progression will look like the following diagram:

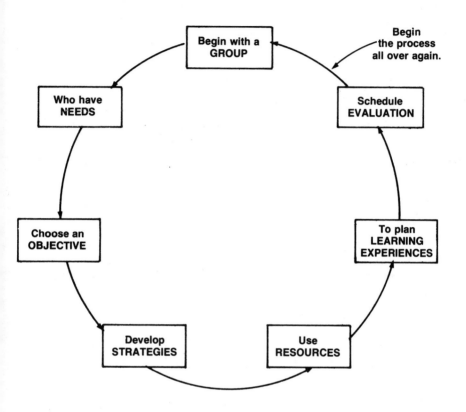

Understanding Groups 7

Group work specialists have discovered that groups, like individuals, have personalities. If you think about it, you will realize that this is true of the groups to which you belong. Some groups seem open and friendly. You seldom feel like a stranger in them for very long. Other groups are intent on getting a job done and seem to value you only if you help with the task. Other groups seem to have no purpose and little concern for each other; they fall apart very easily. Still other groups seem to be made up of a lot of little groups or cliques.

If we are able to determine what factors lead to the development of a group's personality, we can influence these factors and help groups take on the kind of shape which enables them to facilitate growth among members. We can help a group become a caring group which emphasizes the Christian values of individual worth and concern for one another.

There are some very technical names for the factors which influence a group's personality and, like many other areas we have discussed, whole books have been written about them. In this section we will simply get a brief overview of what these factors are and learn some ways of influencing them to develop a caring group.

THE CLIMATE

We can feel the group climate just as we can feel humidity, heat, frost, and wind in the out-of-doors. The climate of a group is the overall feeling that permeates the room when the group is meeting.

It can be:

competitive	or	**cooperative**
people jockeying for position, trying to outtalk or outthink each other, possibly some actual physical confrontation, rewarding persons who contribute the most		people building on each other's ideas, supporting persons who are timid, planning together, working as a team, rewarding those who are good team members
hostile	or	**supportive**
not open to new members, making "mean" comments about present members, angry, aggressive		making new members feel welcome, helping each member find a place, sympathetic when persons fail
inhibited	or	**open**
dependent on one or two leaders to make decisions, not able to carry on a discussion, quiet		leadership moves around the group, discussions are vibrant and alive, ideas flow fast and free, sometimes noisy

You have probably concluded from these descriptions that the climate which is most healthy and which produces a caring group is a climate with the characteristics on the right. You are correct. A group that can be cooperative, supportive, and open is one in which members feel at home, free to be themselves, free to grow.

You can help to develop this kind of climate by meeting in a comfortable room, by encouraging members to cooperate on common goals (and making sure these goals are meeting the needs of most of the members of the group), and by being supportive and open yourself. Most of all, you can encourage this kind of group by sharing in leadership, not making all of the decisions yourself, but letting the group as a whole decide where it wants to go.

RELATIONSHIPS

Within a group, people are concerned about the way they relate to one another in at least three areas: their **inclusion** in group activities, the extent to which they can **control** the group's direction, and the level of **affection** they can give and receive from other group members. Most people move progressively through these concerns. They are initially concerned with inclusion, then control, and finally with affection. However, there is quite a bit of movement back and forth in these areas as the group changes and as individuals themselves change. These three areas have been labeled ICA[1] for short.

Inclusion. When we join a new group, we wonder: Who else is here? To whom do I want to relate? Will I be able to say what I want to say? In other words, we wonder if we will be included.

Most new groups—or old groups who take in new members—need to go through experiences which help them become acquainted and help people feel that they are an important part of the group. Some of the exercises given in chapter 1 (pages 12 and 13) help in this. Informal times of recreation, eating, or just being together also help.

Control. Everyone in a group wants to have some influence on the direction the group goes. We want to be able to put out our own ideas and have them accepted, to have other people agree with us, to feel that we're important to the decision-making process of the group.

We can help everyone feel that they have some control over the direction of the group if we encourage the group to operate democratically. In a democratic group, everyone's views are heard and valued, decisions are made either by majority vote or (preferably) by consensus. The adult leader keeps the group from making harmful decisions but does not make all of the decisions for the group. Everyone has some measure of control.

Affection. When we can feel affection for other members of the group and receive affection from them, relationships within a group have really begun to jell. We actually care what happens to other members of the group; and they care about us. We know immediately when persons are absent and we miss them. We look forward to the group meeting, and we share at a very personal level.

There is no way that we can program affection into our group.

[1]This concept was developed by William C. Schutz in his book, *The Interpersonal Underworld* (Palo Alto, Calif.: Science and Behavior Books, Inc., 1967).

But we can encourage it by providing large blocks of time for persons to relate on a personal, intimate level—retreats, worship experiences, and projects on which they work together—and by developing real affection for members of the group ourselves.

We can also encourage affection by providing small groups within a large group in which persons can touch base with a few people and share their deepest concerns. The more relationships a person is subjected to, the less intimate he or she is likely to be. Small groups should be kept to between twelve and fifteen members if we expect real sharing to occur. If members start dropping out or forming cliques, we should question whether we need to structure more times for small groups to meet.

STAGES OF GROUP DEVELOPMENT

Just as children go through several stages as they grow to maturity, groups go through several stages as they mature.

Stage 1: Dependence. A new group will be dependent on the designated leader (usually the adult) for direction. There will be little participation unless the leader encourages it.

Stage 2: Reaction. The second stage of development can be a rather negative experience unless we are prepared for it. A new group normally goes through a period in which there is a struggle for control. There may be concern about "organizing" or "electing officers." There may be some rejection of the designated leader. Some persons may even reject the group and leave.

Stage 3: Coordination. During this phase, the group works on healing any wounds that emerged during the second stage. Members accept responsibility for the life of the group. Everyone seems to care what happens.

Stage 4: Integration. This is the mature phase of a group when members are able to grow, to change their attitudes and ideas. From this stage, the group moves away from exclusive concern about themselves to a healthy balance between concern for tasks outside the group and concern for their own group.

Knowing that these stages normally occur is very important to us as leaders. We will not expect too much interaction in a group which is in the dependence stage. We will not be too alarmed at interpersonal struggles during the second stage. And we will not expect a group to move out to serve others in significant ways until it has reached the final stage.

We can help a group be a caring group at each stage without inhibiting its normal development. For example, we can provide a positive model of leadership in stage one, trying to meet the needs of the group as we perceive them. At stage two, we can encourage honest confrontation within a context of caring. We can help the group at stage three keep from becoming cliquish and too self-centered, moving them on to stage four and concern for others.

We should caution that groups do not move from stage one to stage four and remain in comfortable maturity for the rest of their lives as a group. There are many influences on groups: new members join, leadership changes, the group's task becomes routine. All of these influences cause groups to move back and forth between the various stages of development. It is helpful, however, to identify these stages so we can see where a group is at a given time and know where it might go.

CHARACTERISTICS OF A CARING GROUP

We have tried to point out in the above discussion the traits which lead to a group personality which is caring, open, involved, and supportive. These can be summarized as:

- A group in which "who I am" is more important than "what I can do."
- A group where I can open myself to others and let them open themselves to me.
- A group where I can learn to care and express this caring.
- A group where I can find support for my mission in the world.

We are not describing a therapy group, although some of these elements may be present in such a group. We are describing a group of healthy individuals who meet together to support each other and to grow in the Christian faith.

This may sound like such a harmonious, caring group that the question may arise: Can such a group do anything or will they spend all of their time thinking about each other?

It is true that the group we have described is not a task-oriented group. They will not "walk all over each other" to achieve a goal. However, if they develop as normal groups do to the level of integration described under the stages of group development, they will be able to accomplish tasks very efficiently. And they will do this while maintaining caring relationships. So our objective is to bring them to this point—and not be impatient while they are moving toward it.

THE LEADER'S ROLE

You may be wondering what your role is in the group

described above, as well as in the planning process described earlier. Actually, this role is never static. It will change as the group changes.

In the early stages of any group's life, you will have a lot of power. Members of the group will look to you for guidance. You will decide what will be studied, what the activities will be, who will be assigned what tasks. Don't be afraid to accept this position of authority initially. The group expects it of you. They are not sure enough of their own abilities or of their acceptance in the group to take leadership roles themselves. You have been designated as the leader and they expect you to fulfill this responsibility.

As the group develops, you will be called upon to fulfill the following functions:

Tell the group what to do. Particularly in the first meeting of the group, you will need to give specific directions about what is taking place. You will have developed the plan for the meeting and will be responsible for carrying ou this plan. (The plan, however, should be based on your knowledge of the group needs and should provide for a high level of group involvement.)

Sell the group on your ideas. When you are not quite sure of where the group can best move, you will come up with ideas and present them as options, but will try your best to sell the group on them. For example, if you are not sure that the group can develop a worship service on its own, you may strongly suggest some good resource materials.

Test your ideas with the group. As you become more sure of resources within the group and know that you can depend on leadership within the group, you will test your ideas with the group and change these ideas if they are rejected by the group.

Consult with the group. When the group has moved to stage three, or coordination, you will depend much more on their ideas. You will ask for their input and the whole group will decide what ideas are accepted.

Join the group. In stage four, integration, you will be seen as a valuable member of the group, but no longer as the authoritative leader. Your ideas will carry no more weight than those of others in the group.

Of course, your role may shift from time to time. Even when the group has reached stage four in its development, there may be times when you will need to tell them what to do or sell your ideas. But your ultimate goal is to be a contributing member of the group. You will always be an adult member—contributing out of your experience as an adult—but you will seldom take over or use your power as leader to manipulate the direction in which the group goes.

As a contributing member of the group, you may be called upon to fulfill any of the following functions which contribute to group life:

Initiate activity. You will help the group get started, define problems, suggest solutions to problems.

Seek information. You will ask for clarification of ideas which have been proposed, request additional information or facts.

Seek opinions. Try to help the group find out what persons think or feel.

Give opinions. You will give your own opinion on subjects discussed; state what your beliefs are.

Elaborate. You will clarify points made by others, try to help the group imagine how a proposal would work if adopted.

Coordinate. You will try to pull together ideas and suggestions so that they build on each other; try to draw together the activities or ideas of various subgroups or members.

Summarize. You will organize the ideas of the group so it knows what it has said.

Test workability. You will examine the practicality and workability of ideas, helping the group test its ideas in real situations.

It is important to realize that in stage four of group development, and even earlier, any group member may assume any of the above roles. You will hopefully only take on the roles which are missing. For example, any member of the group may initiate an idea or summarize information or seek information. However, if someone else doesn't do this when it is needed, you should fill the role.

It is difficult to illustrate how this might be done without printing the entire transcript of a group meeting so you can see what roles are filled and how the leader becomes a part of the group in filling the missing role. To help you understand this further, I would suggest that you tape-record a group session in a group which is in stage four. This could be a peer group to which you belong, or it could be the youth group with which you work if they are far enough along in their development. As you listen to the tape recording, try to identify what role each person is taking. See if there are any roles missing. Would it have been helpful to have someone coordinate ideas or ask for more information? If so, as leader, you could have done this. Such an exercise will sharpen your skills in knowing when to come into a group's discussion and what role to fill in order to move the group to its objective.

CHANGING YOUR LEADERSHIP STYLE

Most of us tend to lead as we were led, and for most of us, that means an authoritative style. We are used to classrooms in which the adult teacher made all of the decisions, provided all of the input, determined the direction in which the class moved.

To move to a more democratic style of leadership in which we are a member of the group is difficult. We need to force ourselves to break out of the mold, to be comfortable with an image other than that of adult authority, to try different roles in a group. There is no easy way to accomplish this. It is simply a risky, trial-and-error process. The way can be smoothed, however, by participating in training sessions in which others are also attempting the same thing. Such training sessions are often held by national and regional church education agencies.

Once we've accomplished the transition, we'll find that we enjoy our participation in the group much more. We don't have to take sole responsibility for the success or failure of the group. We don't have to do all of the planning, think of all of the ideas, maintain all of the discipline. We are sharing leadership with the rest of the group and everyone comes out ahead.

SUMMARY

Much of what we do in youth ministry is done in groups. So it is important to understand how groups function and how we can encourage the development of a caring group in which individuals can mature in their Christian faith.

We should be concerned about the climate of our group, encouraging cooperation, support, and openness, rather than competition, hostility, and dependence on one or two leaders.

Our group members will be concerned with their inclusion in group activities, the kind of influence or control they have in the group, and the affection they give and receive from other members. We can facilitate positive levels of inclusion, control, and affection by spending a lot of time on relationships within the group and by helping the group make decisions democratically.

Our group will move through four stages as it approaches maturity: dependence, reaction, coordination, and integration. We should be aware of these stages of development and not expect an immature group to act as a mature one would. Also, we can encourage caring relationships at each stage of development.

Our goal is to develop a redemptive group which accomplishes the church's mission, but does this while maintaining caring relationships.

As leaders, we will find our role shifting as the group moves through its stages of development. In the beginning we will take a strong authoritarian role, but we will gradually move from this into a shared leadership role in which we "fill in the gaps" in the normal group functions. We can move to this shared leadership role by participating in training sessions and by simple trial and error.

Groups are important in youth ministry, and our leadership of groups is the key to their effectiveness.

Teaching Methods for the 8 Experienced Leader

As an inexperienced leader, you used a few teaching methods, such as the ones we discussed in the second chapter. These were your survival kit methods. With them you could get through a class session or youth meeting with moderate success.

In time, however, you will find these methods limiting. It's like eating the food you can carry in a backpack—it tastes okay on the trail, but you wouldn't want it as a steady diet. There are times when you crave a good lobster or need a fresh fruit.

In addition, your group will need a greater variety of learning activities. You will find that it is hard to meet their needs with your limited repertoire of teaching skills. The following pages will provide you with more teaching methods which can be used as your leadership skill increases. At the end of this section we will describe when these methods should be used to achieve your learning objectives.

A LEARNING PROCESS

Before getting into the actual teaching methods, it might be helpful to present a process which can be used with all of these methods.

The following questions should be asked following the use of any method described on the next few pages.

What? What happened? What did the film or TV program show? What was the content of the story or biblical passage? What new information or ideas did you gather from exposure to the content?

So what? What is the meaning of the experience? What did you discover about yourself, about the Bible, about the Christian faith? It is important to verbalize this meaning. You can't assume that everyone has found meaning in an experience unless he or she is able to articulate it.

Now what? How will this meaning change your behavior, your ideas, your beliefs? What will happen to you as a result of this experience? Again, it is important for learners to verbalize changes so they can commit themselves to these changes.

AN ASSORTMENT OF TEACHING METHODS

The methods covered in this section are not presented in any particular order, indicating a progression in terms of the skill required to use them. They also do not represent an exhaustive listing of teaching methods. Books have been written with more complete lists.[1] This is simply a random listing of some of the more useful teaching methods which are appropriate to youth ministry.

You might want to use this section as you would use a cookbook or manual on carpentry. Select the method you want to use, look it up in this chapter, develop skill in using it, and try it out with your group.

Using Movies, Filmstrips, Slides, Pictures, Tapes, TV

The above media can be lumped together because the process for dealing with them is pretty much identical. They should be used primarily to provide input or to evoke feelings. For example, you would use a movie about growing up to help youth identify what normally happens during this period and to encourage them to express their feelings about the problems of growing up. The same applies to the other media. (Incidentally, the TV we are talking about here is instructional television— programs on educational channels or video discs and tapes which are commercially produced for educational purposes. Some churches have access to equipment which makes the use of these materials viable.)

Before viewing a movie, filmstrip, slides, flat pictures, TV, or listening to an audio cassette, determine why you are using it. What is the learning objective for your session? What do you want it to accomplish? Then make a list of things to look for or listen to as the medium is being shown or heard. This helps group members sharpen their powers of observation and hearing.

When the showing or hearing is over, spend time discussing the content. We will describe this process in relation to a film. **First, ask for general reactions and feelings.** Ask, "What character

[1]See *40 Ways to Teach in Groups* by Martha Leypoldt (Valley Forge: Judson Press, 1967).

affected you most? Why? What part of the film did you like best? Least? Why? What were some of the moods you felt during the film?"

Next, talk about specific feelings. Ask viewers to recall some of their feelings during the film. At what points did they have these feelings? Can they identify why? **Then discuss general themes.** Ask viewers to describe in a sentence or two what the film was about. Ask if they saw any biblical themes. How would they have ended the film differently?

Finally, apply the learnings from the film to the everyday lives of the viewers. How might viewing this film change their behavior or their thinking?

Be sure always to use a film, filmstrip, etc., because it will help you achieve your objective for a learning session not because you have come unprepared for a meeting and it's a good fill-in. Also, be prepared for and allow plenty of time for discussion. This is where real learning takes place.

Using Mass Media

There are times when a film is showing at the local theater or a special is appearing on TV which fits into the course of study in which you are involved. You should take advantage of such mass media as well as others which are readily available: novels, magazine articles, records.

The procedure for using mass media is essentially that outlined above for using educational films, filmstrips, etc. The important thing, again, is to use the medium because it helps you meet a learning objective and to allow plenty of time for discussion afterward.

One caution should be raised about selecting mass media for a learning experience. Be careful either to read an adequate review or, preferably, to review the medium yourself before using it, in order to be sure that it meets your objective. We recommend reviews in *Mass Media* or *Cultural Information Service* (see ordering information in the Resource section, page 126).

Creative Bible Study

In the first chapter, we gave some general procedures for Bible study. The following are adaptations of these procedures.

Multiple Bible Reading. Ask one person to read a passage aloud while the others in the group write down thoughts that come to mind as the passage is read—descriptive words, phrases, ideas. Then ask a second person to read the passage, perhaps from another translation. Again, other members of the group write down their thoughts. Repeat this until five persons have read the passage aloud. Then compare thoughts. Ask, "Do you have any new understandings about this passage? Any questions? Do you see its relevance to your life today?"

Paraphrasing. Have group members read a biblical passage in one or two translations of the Bible and then rewrite the passage in their own words. (You might read the same passage in *The Living Bible* to illustrate what a paraphrase is.) After the paraphrases have been completed, ask, "Why did you use the words you did? What new insights into the meaning of this passage did this process provide?"

Writing in New Forms. Choose a narrative portion of Scripture, such as the story of the feeding of the five thousand, and ask students to rewrite it as a poem, a letter, an historical account, a short story. Discuss the difference in the interpretation of this passage when it is written in these forms. This should give some insight into the need for knowing the literary form when engaging in biblical study.

Creative Expression. Ask youth to use art materials to express the meaning of a passage of Scripture. Use some of the creative expression techniques suggested under this heading on pages 75 and 76. When they have finished, ask each person to comment on his or her creation, showing what meaning was discovered in the biblical passage.

Experiencing the Bible. Ask students actually to live out some of the stories in the Bible. For example, have them read the parable of the talents (Matthew 25:14-29). Then give every group member different amounts of money and tell them to use it as they wish but to return either the original amount or more money earned with the money they were given, in two weeks.

Informal Drama. Dramatize some of the stories from the Bible, writing your own script. The dramatization can either be literal—following the dialogue in the Bible—or you can make it contemporary. You might photograph the dramatization and make a slide set to tell the story.

Writing a Commercial. Write and produce a one-minute commercial which gives the meaning of a brief passage of Scripture, such as the two great commandments. You will find that a lot of thought will go into condensing this meaning into a one-minute presentation that catches the attention of people today.

One word of caution should be given in relation to the use of all of the above methods. You should always approach biblical study from the perspective outlined in chapter 2. Never study a passage out of context or try to make it mean something it was never intended to mean. Never use the above methods as gimmicks to get the attention of the class. Use them only when they help you achieve your learning objective.

Simulation Games

Simulation games are comparatively new learning tools, but they have achieved tremendous popularity, particularly in church education. There are a vast number of simulation games available, and it is possible even to create your own.

A simulation game is actually an extended role play which is competitive and which is carried out in an environment which simulates an actual life situation. For example, one simulation game called the "Road Game" has participants divided into four teams who must draw roads on a playing board which is divided into four blocks. Each team owns one of the blocks, and it must give permission for persons from the other teams to cross its territory. This permission must be given by the team as a whole, who reaches a consensus decision each time a request comes to it. The object is to build as many roads as possible from your territory to the outside edge of the game board within a time limit. After the game is over, players discuss how they made decisions under the pressure of competition and how they cooperated within their team. There can be many learnings about the way they relate with other people, what cooperation is all about, even some application to political questions, particularly feelings about enemies.

There are a number of sources of simulation games. For an introduction to the field, we suggest *Learning Through Simulation Games* by Philip H. Gillispie (New York: Paulist Press, 1974). You can create your own simulation games by using the procedure illustrated in the Appendix, pages 121 and 122.

A simulation game has learning value only when a great deal of time (at least forty-five minutes to an hour) is allotted to discuss it. (This means that most simulation games cannot be used in the normal youth class or youth group time of an hour to an hour and a half. You will need two to three hours for most games. Time is needed for preparing the group, for playing the game, and for drawing learnings at the end.)

In the discussion at the end of the game, concentrate first on feelings. (They will probably be high!) Let players ventilate their feelings so they can look rationally at their learnings. Then discuss learnings—new insights, new concepts, changed behavior. Be sure to apply any learning to situations in the real world. Not every player will be able to make this application without help.

Creative Expression

Creative expression helps youth release feelings, like anger or joy; understand problems, like poverty or their place in the world; and develop group togetherness—if the group as a whole works on a creative project.

Youth respond very enthusiastically to opportunities to create when these opportunities fit into the objectives of their learning experiences. Here are some ideas for creative expression:

Collage. A collage is simply an assortment of magazine pictures, words, perhaps scraps of material, all pasted on a large sheet of newsprint or poster board with edges overlapping. It can be used to illustrate a concept, such as the mission of the church, problems with parents, etc.

Sculpture. Untrained sculptors can work with such things as modeling clay, wire, pipe cleaners, boxes, soda cans, or any other material which can be used to create a three-dimensional piece. Sculpting can be used to illustrate feelings, such as love, concern over the future, one's place in the group.

Painting and Drawing. Nearly everyone knows how to draw a little—at least stick figures or abstract shapes. Use pen and ink, charcoal, pastels, water colors, tempera paint. Painting and drawing can be used to illustrate either feelings or intellectual concepts.

Finger Painting. Youth enjoy finger painting, especially when they can get down on the floor to do it. Try darkening the room, lighting a candle, and doing finger painting to music. Finger paint can be made from liquid starch to which tempera paint or vegetable dye has been added. This is an excellent activity for illustrating deep feelings which cannot easily be put into words.

Writing Poetry, Prose, Drama, Music. Creative writing is a natural creative activity for youth. Poetry especially seems to appeal to adolescents. You will probably not be an expert in helping them with the technical details of writing in any of the above forms, but you can inspire them to write by providing a relaxed setting, some beginning ideas, some resources. You can also get them into a creative mood by doing some imagination exercises. Have them imagine what they would dream if they could create their own dreams. Have them imagine what a rock would say if it could talk. Have them imagine who they would be if they could be anyone.

A special word about writing music. Many youth are skilled in writing lyrics to songs, but few know how to do musical notation. To get around this problem, provide a tape recorder which can record the melody someone sings or plays on the piano. A person skilled in notation can then transcribe it from the tape.

Slides, Movies, Photographs, Cassettes. Youth are usually quite challenged by a project involving the making of slides, an 8mm movie, snapshots, or a cassette recording. Directions for creating these media are in the section on creating resources, pages 85 to 87.

Such projects can be very useful in gathering data about a problem in your community, in illustrating a story or biblical narrative, or in providing content for a worship experience.

Some final words about creative expression as a method. There are times when expressing oneself is an end in itself—particularly when you want to provide an opportunity for persons to get out their feelings. However, in order to learn through creative expression, the creative production must be discussed. If persons have made a collage of world problems, they should share their collages with the total group and identify the problems they have illustrated.

Values Clarification

A number of educators, led by Sidney Simon, have developed some techniques for helping students identify their values, in the hope that they will then be able to change these values or consistently act on them. (Values are defined as beliefs on which we act.) These techniques are directly related to our objectives in church education.

A number of these techniques can be found in the book *Values Clarification: A Handbook of Practical Strategies for Teachers and Students* by Simon, Howe, and Kirschenbaum (New York: Hart Publishing Co., Inc., 1972).

Also, a number of the strategies have been adapted for church education and can be found in such resources as *Respond* (*Volumes 1, 2, 3, 4, and 5,* Valley Forge: Judson Press) and in the book

Integrating Values by Louis M. Savary (New York: Cebco Pflaum, 1974). The ladder technique we described on page 56 of chapter 6, illustrated in the Appendix, page 120, is an example of an adaptation of a value clarification technique.

In using values clarification techniques, you should keep in mind that you are not trying to impose your own values upon members of your group—or impose the values of the church. Rather, you are trying to get youth to clarify the values they presently hold—to put these out in the open to see if they want to keep them or change them. Most people are genuinely surprised at some of the values they hold. Your objective will be to help them get over this surprise and live consistently with a set of Christian values they can affirm.

Human Relations Training

Human relations training embodies a whole series of methods which can be used to help persons relate better with each other and to help groups function more effectively.

For example, there are exercises which can help persons in a group develop more trust in each other, exercises which can help individuals communicate more effectively, exercises which can help group members become acquainted very quickly. A number of these exercises are given in the Appendix under Group Growth Exercises (page 122). Additional exercises can be found in resources listed in the Bibliography.

In using human relations training, as with most other teaching methods, you should first try the exercise yourself so you are comfortable using it with others. Try it with some friends or with the planning committee for your group. Discover how effectively it works with you. Then you will be in a better position to use it effectively with members of your group.

Also, be sure to allow plenty of time for discussion of feelings after using a human relations exercise. Usually, at least a half hour should be devoted to such discussion. Use the process described on page 70: "What? So what? Now what?"

Finally, I like to make participation in human relations exercises voluntary. Some persons are not ready to work on group growth or personal relational skills. I do not like to force them into the process until they are ready. (This is true for most learning activities, but particularly human relations training.)

Continued on page 82

CHART OF METHODS*

METHOD	DESCRIPTION OF METHOD	VALUES
Audio-Visual	This is a method which uses eye and ear gates for communicating ideas. It includes sound films, sound filmstrips, and recordings used with pictures.	Presents facts in a rememberable way; makes the inaccessible accessible.
Brainstorming	Ideas are expressed in a climate of complete freedom. ANY idea is accepted; NO judgments are expressed about an idea. The subject matter is described, and everyone expresses any and all ideas that come to mind. A time limit is prescribed at the beginning. ALL ideas are recorded by a secretary.	Creates a climate of free expression by removing the threat of judgment; specializes on ideas only, so everyone can "think up a storm."
Buzz Groups	The total group is divided into smaller groups (3 to 6 in each) to provide an opportunity for reaction to a problem, lecture, audiovisual, or other presentation. Buzz groups can be formed by clustering or by counting off. Discussion should be limited to not more than five to six minutes. Reports should be made to total group, reassembled.	Provides time and climate for every person to state ideas, ask questions, and think through the question; gets 100% participation.
Creative Expression	The group feelings and ideas through original art: sculpture, painting, wiring, etc.	Feelings are allowed to be expressed openly; ideas are more clearly understood as they are expressed in nonverbal forms.
Directed Reading	Assignments for simultaneous reading are written on a flipchart or chalkboard. Participants pair off to read together silently or aloud and to discuss the reading in relation to the subject.	Assures that every participant reads the resource material essential to group discussion.
Discussion	Ideas are shared orally in a group. The group should be small (15 maximum, if possible). All participants should be able to make eye contact with each other. Each participant's accepting responsibility for everyone to express themselves is important.	Draws ideas from the experiences of all participants and helps develop areas of agreement.
Field Trip	A group visits a setting(s) other than its normal meeting place, usually to investigate a problem or to confront group with a real situation.	Provides opportunity for a group to secure firsthand knowledge or confront a real situation related to or stimulating a subject of group study or action.

*This chart is not comprehensive, either in the methods listed or in their uses.

Adapted from Learning About Methods by D. Allison Holt, a pamphlet produced by the Christian Board of Publications, St. Louis, Mo. Used with permission.

LIMITATIONS	EXAMPLES	
	WHEN TO USE	WHEN NOT TO USE
Easily construed as entertainment; must be expertly done or it loses its value; equipment failure is a hazard.	When a group needs a living experience from outside the life of the group.	If the illustration portrayed is beyond the need of the group; if obtaining the film in time to be useful is difficult.
Produces a lot of apparently unusable material, thus making some people feel it has been a waste of time.	When a group is ready to be extremely creative, daring, and adventuresome; when it is up against a blank wall and needs new ideas.	If a group already has come to a final decision, for this process could very well upset the work that has been done.
Ideas are likely to be shallow and disorganized, due to the shortness of time.	When everyone has the urge to talk; when group members seem to be stymied or reluctant to express their ideas.	If the group has moved into deep discussion or is dealing in technical matters that do not need opinions.
Requires art materials and sufficient time, as well as an open, accepting learning environment.	When group members need to release feelings; when personal opinions about ideas need to be shared in a nonthreatening way.	When persons seem unwilling to express themselves; when facilities are limited.
Difficult to time because some people are slow readers, others very fast; difficult for some pairs to stick to subject being covered.	When a group comes together and it is obvious they have not had a chance to read ahead of time.	When the reading material is limited (just a few copies of the book); when it appears that everyone has read the assignment.
Limited to small groups (15); more aggressive persons can dominate; discussion cannot be hurried if it is to be fruitful.	When personal opinions and illustrations are needed; when differences of opinions and agreements need to be expressed.	If the group is in need of accurate, technical, detailed information.
Requires extra time and energy for planning; may have to be scheduled at a time inconvenient to some group members.	When it provides the group the best means of obtaining accurate information, insights, or feelings about a subject that will help achieve the group goal.	When leader is ill-prepared; when members are not aware of purpose of the trip; when trip is seen only as something to do, and little or no planning for learning is made.

Chart of Methods, continued

	DESCRIPTION OF METHOD	VALUES
Human Relations Training	A variety of experiences are provided through which group members learn to relate more effectively.	Provides opportunities for learning new behavior and practicing relational skills in an accepting environment; facilitates rapid group development.
Lecture	A carefully prepared oral presentation of a subject is made by a qualified person. This is one person presenting a set of ideas, either memorized or read, to a group of listeners.	Communicates a body of material in an orderly, logical, and factual fashion; makes listening an art.
Panel (Panel-Forum)	A group of four to eight persons who have special knowledge of the topic sit at a table in front of the audience and hold an orderly and logical conversation on the assigned subject, guided by a moderator. (It becomes a panel-forum if the audience directs questions to panel.) The moderator closes with a summary.	Brings a variety of knowledge—agreements and disagreements—to the group; audience can identify with various panel members.
Resource Person	A person who has extensive knowledge of a subject is called upon to provide the knowledge the group needs. He or she gives the facts and does not seek to promote a soapbox or to thwart group creativity.	Provides the wisdom of someone who "has been there"; helps group test its ideas against real experience.
Role Play	A group of "players" acts out a given situation dealing with a specific problem confronting the group. It includes these steps: select the situation; assign roles; brief the players and the group; enact the situation; cut; interview some of the observing group and the players; summarize the findings; "de-role" the players.	A non-threatening way of dealing with emotional situations; authentic because it is spontaneous, never rehearsed.
Simulation Game	A life situation is simulated in a competitive game.	Forces participants to discover how they really act.
Values Clarification	Various techniques are used to help group members identify their values.	When values are identified, they can be changed or acted on consistently.

LIMITATIONS	EXAMPLES	
	WHEN TO USE	WHEN NOT TO USE
Sometimes application is not made between the classroom experience and life situations; requires skilled leadership.	When a new group forms; when a group or individuals face relational problems.	When time for dealing with emerging feelings is limited; when skilled leadership is not available.
Audience cannot complete its participation—only listen; easy for persons to get lost in their own thoughts.	When a unified message is needed; when one person is an authority on a subject and can be stimulating.	Only if audience participation is needed, in which case it can be used in conjunction with other methods.
Easy for panel members to ramble if they are not thoroughly oriented to the subject.	To introduce a new topic; to help a stymied group regain its perspective by considering different views of a subject in an orderly and logical conversation.	If a group is assembling for the first time; if the members have had a thoroughly satisfying discussion of the subject.
Possibility of creating dependence on a "headliner" to provide the answers.	When a group is in need of an experienced voice; when a group feels the need to find out what others are doing.	If the group members have not really thought through their own position on the matter.
Tendency to let the role play become entertainment or to feel it is fictitious and so not of value, to forget that the emotions ARE real.	When a group needs to have some real data about its own life, not something from outside itself.	If a group is extremely tired and its emotions seem on edge, a role play could easily get out of hand.
Requires two to three hours; must be thoroughly discussed; brings out strong feelings.	When a group needs to examine behavior or experience solving a problem such as energy conservation, poverty, hunger.	When members might be threatened by looking at their behavior; when time is limited.
Must be used by persons who are accepting of other persons' values and not intent on imposing their own value system.	When a group needs to discover their present values.	When members are unable or unwilling to face inconsistencies in their value system.

HOW TO SELECT LEARNING METHODS

The methods discussed in this chapter are typically used in youth resource materials. We have described them here as a way of acquainting you with the "how" of using them. There may be times, however, when you will need to know some criteria for selecting among the various methods available.

The best learning method will be the method which will help you achieve your goal. For example, if you want your class to learn a skill, such as how to study the Bible, you will need to use a learning method which will help them become acquainted with the skill (perhaps input on cassettes or in a filmstrip) and an opportunity to practice the skill (like writing a play based on an interpretation of a particular passage of the Bible).

If you are trying to change attitudes, you might want to use values clarification or simulation games which help the students evaluate their present attitudes—the first step in changing them. If you are trying to teach concepts, such as faith, a movie might illustrate the concept in concrete form and creative expression (such as creating a collage) might help them illustrate their understanding of the concept. If you are teaching facts, a lecture might be helpful, or a filmstrip or other audiovisual. The accompanying chart spells this out in detail.

SUMMARY

As you develop more experience in youth leadership, you will feel the need to increase your repertoire of teaching skills. You will want to learn to use the methods described in this chapter in order more effectively to meet the needs of your group.

Most of these methods are commonly used in youth ministry resources. As you come across them, look up the description of the way to use them which is given in this chapter. Use the chapter like a cookbook or manual on carpentry.

In addition, there may be times when you will want to design your own learning session rather than follow the step-by-step plan outlined in your resource material. The chart showing when each method can effectively be used will help you know which method to select to achieve your learning objective.

The learning process described on pages 70 and 71 will help you use all of these methods effectively and it is an easy formula to remember: What? So what? Now what?

Resources | 9

"How can I find the right resource for my group?" "What's new in resources?" "Why doesn't someone produce a resource for the small church—the inner-city church—the ethnic church?" "Why can't we find a resource which can be used without a lot of preparation?"

These are all questions which are raised by youth leaders as they struggle with the whole area of resources. The answers, unfortunately, are not easy. It takes time and skill to find appropriate resources, adapt them to your special needs, even create your own resources. But these skills are essential for effective youth ministry.

This chapter will help you discover what resources are, how to choose them, and how to create your own. You will also discover how you can keep up-to-date on new resources so you have the "right" resource at your fingertips.

A DEFINITION OF RESOURCES

We are not defining resources only as printed materials, such as the curriculum resource you use in your church school or the program book you use with your youth group. A resource is any source of information which can be used to support a learning experience. It can be a book, a film, an audio cassette, a person, an agency in the community, a building, a library. Try not to limit your sights to the material with which you are provided. Try to recycle resources—find new ways to use old materials. Try to find a use for unlikely resources—a Coke can (it can be bent into a sculpture), a Twister game (it can be transformed into a simulation game), the oldest member of your congregation (a good source of historical information).

To stretch your imagination in defining resources, make a list of all of the resources that are present in your community. You may be surprised at how extensive the list is, even if you live in a small community. Don't forget the resources available through your local school or through the various places of employment of your church members.

SELECTING RESOURCES

The most important consideration in selecting a resource is whether or not it will help you achieve your objective. Do not select a resource before you have gone through the planning process outlined in chapter six: determine the needs of your group, write an objective, and develop strategies before selecting resources. Your resources will help you carry out your strategies to meet your objective.

But which resource should you choose to achieve your objective? How can you discriminate between the vast variety of resources which are available? Here are some criteria:

● **Is the resource theologically acceptable and educationally sound?** Is it based on a theology which is consistent with your own? By this, we do not mean that it should only present beliefs with which you agree, but that the theological framework should be one with which you are comfortable. (For example, a theology which stresses a church which is open only to those who accept a narrow list of beliefs would not be acceptable if you believe people should be able to express a wide range of religious beliefs.)

Are the educational principles ones with which you feel comfortable? If you believe students should be actively involved in learning experiences instead of subjected to lectures, is this provided for in the material?

● **Is the resource one which will appeal to your group and respond to their needs?** Is it designed for their age level? Is it culturally acceptable? If you are working with an ethnic group, will it appeal to their particular concerns? Is it a resource which they enjoy? (Have they seen too many filmstrips recently or gone on too many field trips?) Is it within their range of abilities? Does it meet their needs for growth?

● **Is the resource one with which you can feel comfortable as a leader?** You should not be limited to resources which provide activities with which you have had some experience. However, do not plan to use new activities unless you have time to practice them before using them. For example, if you have never used a simulation game, do not plan to use one until you have done a dry run with some friends.

• **Is the resource financially feasible?** Some resources are more expensive than others, and you may find that your budget does not permit your using them. However, we should raise a caution here. In considering the cost of a resource, think of the length of time it may be used and its level of effectiveness. A filmstrip may be expensive initially, but it can be used for several years. A film may be expensive to rent, but its effectiveness might be worth the extra expense. You might also consider whether you can borrow some resources from your community library or from other churches.

CREATING RESOURCES

There are times when the unavailability of the right resource makes it imperative for you to create your own resource. For example, if you are studying social problems in your community, it might be necessary to make a film to document some of these problems or to interview representatives of social agencies with a cassette tape recorder. There are other times when making your own resource gets members of your group more involved in the study—as they create the resource, they pick up facts and attitudes that are learnings in themselves.

It is impossible to provide instructions for creating every resource in the space we have available here. Instead, we have selected a few resources which are easily created and not too time consuming.

The first step in creating any new resource is to plan it, using the planning process outlined in chapter 3. Collect data about what is already known concerning the subject, about the audience who will be using the resource, and facts about the subject itself. Organize this data, selecting the most relevant information, and then write your objective. The creation of the resource will then proceed as strategy. The following are technical instructions for creating various resources:

Camera-less Slides

Cut a two-inch square of clear contact paper. Remove the backing and place it over a picture of the same size in a magazine. (The magazine must be printed on clay-based paper. Wet your finger and rub it across the ink; if the ink comes off, the paper is clay-based.) Press down the contact paper with a blunt instrument, like a spoon, so that no air bubbles appear.

Soak the square in hot water to which a few drops of detergent have been added. In a few minutes, the paper can be removed from the contact paper and you will find that the ink has been transferred to the contact paper. Remove the square from the water, let dry, and then back it with another piece of clear contact paper. Mount in a slide mount, available from camera supply stores.

Audio Tape Cassettes

Many youth have cassette tape recorders. Use one to produce an interview or a musical recording or recording of a speech, drama, or role play.

In interviewing, it is important to have your questions written out in advance—not to follow religiously, but to provide some structure for the interview and to keep from having long pauses when you are trying to think of something to say.

When taping the interview, use a hand microphone and hold it approximately six inches from the mouth of the person who is speaking (including yourself when you are asking questions).

If you wish to edit a taped interview, you can do it in two ways. The easiest is to link it to a second tape recorder with a patch cord. Then play only the parts you want to keep on a new tape in the second recorder. It is also possible to edit a cassette tape by splicing it. Secure a kit for this from your audio supply dealer.

In taping music, make sure that you tape directly from a phonograph, using a patch cord. If you use a microphone placed in front of the phonograph speakers, you are likely to pick up motor noise as well as other extraneous noises.

8mm Film

You can make your own film with an 8mm camera by following these guidelines:
- Do not move when you are shooting. Let the subject do the moving.
- Take a variety of shots for each major idea:
   long shots: the full scene or full person
   medium shots: medium between long shot and close-up; waist to head of person
   close-up: main object fills frame; head and shoulders of person

• Take some cutaway shots (shots of related subjects, such as a person watching the main action) and cut-in shots (shots that cut into the main action, such as close-up of hands) to use in editing.

• Shoot some scenes from two different perspectives.

• When shooting scenes of moving persons or objects, the movement should always be shot in the same direction. (Ex.: The person walks from right to left in each scene.)

The real work in creating an 8mm film is in the editing. You should have five or six times the film you will actually use in the final product. Use a film editor which is available from your camera supply store. Here is the process for editing:

• Project the entire film. Make a numbered list of all scenes. Then note which scenes you want to have in your final film and which you will cut altogether. Make a list of the scenes as they will appear in the edited film.

• Break the roll of film down into individual scenes. Label each scene, using numbers from your list. Hang these pieces of film on a wall or table edge in numbered order.

• Now splice all of these scenes together, in order. Run this through the projector and decide which scenes need to be cut. This process will be repeated many times until you come up with a film that is satisfactory.

Overhead Projector Transparencies

If you have access to an overhead projector, you may find this a helpful teaching resource, especially if you can make your own transparencies.

You will need a piece of clear plastic and an opaque pencil or colored transparency pencils. First make a sketch of the drawing, chart, or other material you want to put on the transparency. Then transfer this to the piece of plastic with your pencil. You can make overlays by placing several sheets of plastic together and taping them on alternate sides to the backing sheet.

KEEPING UP-TO-DATE ON RESOURCES

Leaders sometimes complain that they can't find any resources; they just aren't being produced anymore. What these leaders usually mean is they can't find the resource they are looking for, the resource that fits the needs of their group at a particular point in time.

A vast assortment of resources is being produced—both church education resources and public education resources which can be adapted for church use. In fact, so many resources are being produced that several publications are devoted exclusively to reviewing them and denominational educational staffs must devote many hours to keeping abreast of new resources.

The only way you, as a local leader, can keep up with what is available and have the resource you need at your fingertips when you need it is to keep a running file of each new resource you come across which you think has potential for your group. The few minutes that it will take to make up a file card when you first learn of a new resource will save many hours when you are in need of a particular resource later.

Your file should be simple, but contain as much information as necessary to describe the resource and indicate how to order it. I have found a subject file to be the most helpful, using subjects such as the following: Bible study, camping/conferences, career guidance, Christian faith, personal growth, international mission, leader resources, sexuality, social issues, worship.

I then assign a symbol for each medium: B—book, D—drama, F—film, FS—filmstrip, MM—mixed media, P—photo or art print, Ph—pamphlet, R—record, S—slides, SG—simulation game, and T—audio tape.

The information you will need on each card is: subject category, title, author (if given), type of media, technical information (length of film, color or black and white, audio cassette or reel, publisher, etc.), description, and ordering source. Your card will look like this:

PERSONAL GROWTH

To Be a Person (F) 16mm, color, 19 min. Rental: $25.00 from Billy Budd Films, Inc., 235 East 57th St., New York, NY 10022.

A collage of life scenes and comments from youth about what it means to be a person. Covers a wide range of ideas about acceptance, loneliness, being an individual, and pretending to be someone else. Part of the Circle of Life film series.

You can keep up-to-date on new resources by subscribing to periodicals which review these resources. Several are listed in the Appendix, page 126.

SUMMARY

Resources are available or can be made to meet the needs of any group and to help you achieve any learning objective. The effective youth leader is not limited to the printed resources with which he or she has been provided but knows how to discover new resources, recycle resources, and even create new resources. Resources should always be chosen because they help you meet your learning objectives. Their selection should be based on the following criteria: The resource should be theologically acceptable and educationally sound. It should appeal to your group and respond to their needs. It should be one with which the leader feels comfortable. It should be financially feasible.

The secret to having the right resource available to meet emerging needs in your group is keeping up-to-date on new resources. This can be done by keeping a card file of resource ideas.

Resources are keys to an effective youth ministry, but no one resource will meet all of your needs. You must develop the skill of selecting appropriate resources for your group and adapting them to your own special needs.

10 Settings for Learning

As you become better acquainted with youth in your group, you will recognize that no one setting[1] can meet all of their needs for Christian education. The church school class or study group will help them discuss their faith and hopefully practice putting it into action. But the hour or so you have available once a week doesn't allow you to go in depth in any subject. By the next week the interest of your group may have shifted to an entirely different subject.

The camp or conference helps youth to experience community much more than they can in a one-hour meeting each week and to go into greater depth in study. A trip has some values which cannot be found in other settings, as do retreats.

In this chapter we will discuss several settings for church education in which specific needs may be met. We cannot go into detail in any one setting, but further information can be found in the resources listed in the bibliography.

STUDY GROUP

Let's begin with our example above—the study group. This is a place where direct input can be given in an organized way, where youth can research questions, discuss them, express new ideas, develop skills. The traditional study group consists of one or two adult leaders and twelve to fifteen students (any more will limit opportunities for individuals to participate). In some cases, the sessions are planned by a youth and adult planning team and each person takes responsibility for the learning experience. In other cases, the adult leader(s) may do most of the planning.

[1] "Setting" is used to describe a particular type of educational experience. The church school is one setting. Retreats, trips, and conferences are other settings.

You may use a resource book, a film, a role play—any of the learning activities we discussed earlier—to help youth get into faith questions and find answers for themselves. For continuity, the group should meet once a week for an hour to an hour and a half. Everyone moves through the session at the same pace, as a total group. (Even though the large group is sometimes divided into smaller groups, it always comes back together before moving on to the next session.)

LEARNING CENTER

A variation of the traditional study group is the learning center approach. In this setting, several activities take place simultaneously, focusing on a common theme. Each activity is self-instructional; that is, it can be carried out without the help of an adult leader. However, several resource persons (adult or youth) are on hand to provide guidance when it is requested. All persons work at the activity they choose, at their own pace. Individuals define their own objectives by selecting objectives from a list that has been prepared for the session or by working out their objectives with an adult counselor in periodic conferences during the unit.

An example of a learning center is the following:

The group has chosen a unit on death education. They choose the questions they want to work on from a list that has been posted in the room. The list also directs them to the centers where questions may be answered.

In one corner they may watch a filmstrip about the cycle of life. In another corner they may listen to a cassette tape recording of a debate on whether or not there is life after death. In another section of the room they may listen to a popular recording of a song about suicide. Several magazine articles on abortion are provided on a table, along with several books on death. They can watch a filmstrip on the biblical view of death in another spot in the room. Art materials are provided in still another spot for them to express their feelings about the death of someone close. And some cardboard tombstones have been set up in the center of the room where they may write their own epitaphs.

Resource leaders need to be present to help persons get the most out of the materials present and to see if they are answering the questions they chose. The total group may come together at some time to compare learnings and suggest next steps in the unit.

RETREAT

A retreat is an occasion when a group can spend some concentrated time together—living together, studying together, working together, and forming community together. It can take place over a weekend, over one night, or in just one day. It can be used for planning, for studying a subject in depth, for becoming acquainted with each other and strengthening the group ties, or for meditation and worship.

Retreats should be planned with as much care as you plan a study session. Use the planning model given in chapter 3. Set realistic objectives and choose your location with care so that it contributes to your objectives. Plan your schedule in advance, but leave it open to change if needs emerge. The schedule should provide for a balance of work, recreation, and maintenance tasks like cooking and cleaning. Try to keep the costs down as much as possible by taking your own recreational equipment, possibly taking sleeping bags, and driving in car pools.

There may be some legal considerations if you hold a retreat away from the church. Make sure that drivers are insured and that the church carries accident insurance on each individual (this costs very little and is well worth the investment). Get permission from parents for minors to go on the retreat. Also get parents to authorize emergency medical treatment if the parents cannot be reached when such treatment is required.

Some other considerations in planning your retreat are:

● Make sure you have all of your resources with you. (If you are showing a film, do you have a projector, an extra bulb, and a take-up reel?)

● Give clear instructions about the kind of clothing to take as well as sports equipment and musical instruments.

● Be certain that you have good eating facilities. Nothing can ruin the morale of the group faster than inadequate food.

● Explain any regulations relating to the use of the retreat center before going so people are aware of restrictions. Also agree, as a group, on rules which will facilitate your accomplishing your objectives on the retreat, such as attendance, hours, etc.

● Be prepared for youth wanting to stay up late. Work this into your schedule. If it cannot be worked out because it would interfere with others, discuss this in advance and set a curfew. I have found that allowing youth to stay up until one or two o'clock in the morning and setting the opening session at ten the next morning saves a lot of headaches (for you) and yawns (from youth) when you are trying to get into some heavy program material.

CAMPS AND CONFERENCES

Camps and conferences offer the same values as retreats, but they usually take place over a longer period of time. Camps are usually held in out-of-door settings, while conferences are often held at conference centers or on college campuses. Conferences are usually more structured than camps.

Camps and conferences are often scheduled by regional or national church organizations, and you simply recruit youth to attend them. However, you may want to plan your own camp. Think about a canoe trip, backpacking trip, or bike hike as a camping experience. These are unique community-building settings.

INTERGENERATIONAL GROUPS

All of the settings given in this section can be used for intergenerational groups, but we will describe such groups here as a separate kind of setting—one in which adults, youth, and possibly young children meet together to plan their own activities and meet their own goals.

The church is one of the few places in which intergenerational groups can take place today. Most of our other institutions are composed of persons of one generation.

An intergenerational group provides an opportunity for youth and adults to compare their ideas with persons of many experiences and backgrounds. It allows for the sharing of experiences between children, youth, and adults. It helps overcome the communication gap that often exists between generations.

Intergenerational groups take skillful planning. You will need to provide some activities which help persons get to know each other as individuals in order to break down the stereotypes they may have about age groups. Some group growth exercises are good for this. You will also need to provide activities which allow for a wide range of interest and skill.

TRIPS

Many youth groups take trips together during a school vacation or during the summer. Like retreats, these provide an excellent time for community building and depth study.

In planning a trip, have a clear objective in mind. Going to New

York City or Montana or Disneyland is not educational in itself. You need to have a reason for going—even if your reason is just to have fun together. Program into the experience ways of meeting your objective. If you are going to study poverty in New York City, plan some definite times for input and some times to evaluate learnings. Schedule an orientation session before you leave for the trip. Have a reunion-evaluation meeting after you return home.

VOLUNTARY SERVICE

Voluntary service provides a chance for youth to be involved in situations where they can express their faith and share it with others. These projects can be done in several ways. Individuals can sign up with denominational or interdenominational groups. Local churches or regional organizations can plan their own projects. Or youth can volunteer their service in existing organizations in the community, such as hospitals, nursing homes, prisons, or day-care centers.

One of the cardinal rules of voluntary service is that persons should work in local projects before taking part in a project away from home. Learning to live with people they have never met before can take as much work as learning to serve effectively, and the two tasks should be approached at different times.

Voluntary service opportunities should be selected carefully. The project should meet a real need. It should be done with, not for, the persons who are directly benefiting from it. It should make use of skills persons already have or can learn during a training period prior to involvement in the project.

Some kind of orientation should be provided for every voluntary service project. This should cover the kinds of things volunteers might expect to find and to accomplish, any attitudes they will need to change, any specific skills and ways of effectively accomplishing the project. Evaluation should also be a part of each project. If the project is a long-term one, evaluation should be periodic.

INFORMAL SETTINGS

There are many informal settings where Christian education can take place. Sometimes this is the best education. You can meet in a relaxed atmosphere with one individual or a small group and deal with concerns on a very personal level.

Some informal settings are: the drop-in center, the coffeehouse, pizza after school, lunch at school, spontaneous conversations after meetings or in the shopping center. And don't overlook the car pool. Some of my best educational experiences with young teens took place when I was delivering seven or eight youth to their homes after a church event.

INDIVIDUAL COUNSELING

The youth leader is often called upon to provide individual counseling. We cannot go into great detail here on methods for this, but we can list some things to consider.

• Listen more than you talk. It is surprising how many people solve their own problems once they have a chance to verbalize them to a sympathetic listener.

• Ask clarifying questions. Help the individual understand the nature of the problem.

• Concentrate on feelings. Ask, "How does this make you feel?" rather than "What do you think about this?" Feelings reveal much about the source of a problem.

• Don't give advice; present options and let the person solve the problem. Giving advice makes a person dependent on you and also makes you responsible if the advice doesn't work. Help the individual solve the problem by pointing out several optional ways of acting and discussing the possible consequences of each option. Let the person choose the option that appears to be most satisfactory.

• Keep information confidential. Under no circumstances should you report to parents or others any information given to you in a counseling situation. If you feel parents should be involved or if something should come to the attention of legal authorities or a doctor, encourage the individual to take the initiative in this. Offer to go along to the meeting with parents or police or doctor if this would provide the necessary support.

YOUTH MUSIC GROUPS

Youth music groups have become very popular in many churches. There is a great deal of creative religious music being written for such groups, and many opportunities seem to be open for youth participation in worship experiences in their own congregation as well as in other churches on tours.

Music groups provide an excellent setting for developing community. Especially when groups tour together, a real closeness develops among group members. They can also help youth develop confidence in their abilities and provide a way for them to contribute to the life of their church as well as share their faith with others.

However, in order for these values to be present, a youth music group needs to avoid the temptation to place performance before the needs of persons. Certainly a quality performance is to be desired, but this can be accomplished without damaging the self-concepts of individuals, without walking all over people in order to achieve perfection.

Such a group also needs to guard against cliquishness and against the exclusion from the church's ministry of youth who do not choose to participate in a music program. Some churches find that a music group takes so much energy and financial commitment that they are unable to provide programs which meet the needs of youth in their congregation who are not involved in music.

And, as has been said about every other setting, a youth music group should not be organized just because it has become a popular thing to do. It should meet real needs of youth in your church.

CONTEMPORARY WORSHIP

We discussed traditional worship in the first chapter. As you become more secure in your leadership of worship experiences, you may want to expand some of the traditional forms and plan contemporary worship.

Contemporary worship can be informal—that is, it can allow for persons to "break in" with their insights or contributions. It can make use of creative art—banners, unusual worship centers, slides, jazz music, poetry.

Above all, contemporary worship should enable you to be relevant—to meet the needs in your own group, to bring before God the individual concerns and the group celebrations that are unique to your own situation.

You will have to experiment to discover appropriate forms that "fit" your group. You will have to know what popular songs group members are listening to, what headlines in the newspaper are affecting their lives, what they have created that can add to the experience.

It is difficult to describe contemporary worship. You need to experience it to know what it is about. I have been a part of a church which has experimented with contemporary worship in an early service for several years. Sometimes it works and other times it falls flat (which is also true of traditional worship). When it works, I feel involved, a part of a celebrating group, in touch with the divine. There is a movement—a sense of flow—from the concerns I brought with me to new insights and new relationships. There is spontaneity and relevance. There is a feeling that we are all on the same wavelength, bound with an invisible cord of caring.

Here are some guidelines for enabling contemporary worship to take place:

● Begin with a concern, not a theme. Plan the worship around concerns which the worshipers bring with them, enabling them to participate in the experience. A theme tends to make worshipers into spectators rather than participants. If you are planning a Christmas worship service, find out what questions youth are struggling with in relation to Christmas. Are they concerned with the commercialism, with what the "spirit of Christmas" is? Don't just plan a service on "Christmas." Relate it to specific concerns about Christmas.

● Concentrate on the environment. The room should be the kind of place that encourages spontaneity. Rugs on the floor for sitting or chairs in a circle are helpful. The room should also raise questions about your central concern. You might have posters on the walls, gifts as a worship center, Santa Claus ads.

Use popular media as well as traditional. Both have a place in contemporary worship. Use popular songs, quotes from the daily newspaper, current books, films, and records as well as the Bible, traditional liturgy, traditional hymns, and symbols such as the cross.

● Allow for the worshipers to participate physically in the experience. Use some hand-clapping songs. Ask them to do creative movement. Divide into two's to discuss a biblical interpretation. (Note: This participation should always be optional; no one should be coerced into participation. Some people find it impossible to participate in these ways in a worship service. Persons who do not choose to participate physically should be given an opportunity to meditate quietly on their own, to write, or to participate in whatever way they feel comfortable.)

● Be celebrative! Shout out your joy! Release balloons into the sky! Embrace each other! Express your feelings openly.

SELECTING SETTINGS FOR LEARNING

Your objective will determine the kind of setting which will be most effective for your learning experience. We have tried to show the various kinds of objectives which might be met in each of the settings described above.

Some objectives lend themselves to certain settings, even though they might be achieved in others to some degree. For example, you can create a caring group in a church school class if you meet together over a long period of time with the same persons present each week, but a weekend retreat will help you develop a caring group more quickly and efficiently. You can provide input on how to study the Bible on a trip, but not as effectively as you might in a study group.

Refer back to the circular process chart on page 60. Review the progression of the planning process, and you will see that the setting is the last thing you select—after you have developed your objective and decided on your learning activities and resources.

Actually, there are times when your setting will determine your activities and resources—at least influence their selection—but you should not let your choice of setting come first. That is, you should not plan a fall retreat just because you have always had a fall retreat. Decide what your group needs this fall and then decide in what setting it can best be achieved.

SUMMARY

The experienced leader will want to explore a number of learning settings (or educational experiences) in order to discover ones which will most efficiently move the group toward its goal.

If the group is interested in long-term study, for example, the church school class, evening study group, or Saturday morning class may be the best setting. If individuals in the group have different study objectives for the long-term study, the learning center might be an appropriate variation.

When members of a group need to become better acquainted, work on group problems, or study a subject at greater depth, the retreat may be a useful setting.

If there is a need for greater exposure to youth from other communities or to some broader ideas presented by resource persons who are ordinarily not available to the local church, the conference is a helpful setting. Camping, on the other hand, will provide for more intimate relationships and for interaction with physical surroundings.

Intergenerational groups provide opportunities for a broad sharing of ideas among youth, adults, and children. Trips offer exposure to new environments, people, and cultures, plus provide an opportunity for developing a close-knit group. Voluntary service allows for the sharing of faith in concrete action. Informal settings—the drop-in center, lunch at school, conversations at the shopping center—provide casual encounters that nurture relationships. Individual problems can be dealt with through individual counseling. Youth music groups provide an opportunity for youth to express their faith and develop musical skills, as well as experience meaningful fellowship. Contemporary worship gives youth a chance to celebrate their faith, using contemporary media, physical participation, and spontaneous contributions.

Each of the above settings may offer advantages other than the ones we have described. You will want to experiment with each one to determine which settings provide the best opportunities for your group to meet its objectives.

One final reminder: Never select a setting until you have worked through the planning process to the point of choosing an objective. Even though you have been assigned to a particular setting, such as a church school class, take the time to work out your objectives before you begin teaching. You may want to change your church school class into a retreat, an intergenerational group, or a trip. Make settings work for you; don't accept them as rigid structures to which you must adjust as you build your program.

Section 4
The Difficult
Questions

Some Common Leadership Problems 11

Every group is different, and in a lifetime of leadership you may never come across the same problem situation twice. But certain problems seem to occur at one time or another in most groups. This chapter will provide some handles for solving these common problems.

The suggestions given here are based on ways experienced leaders have dealt with similar problems. However, only you can determine what will work in your situation. The best way to do this is to go back to the planning process, outlined in chapter 6. Use this process to plan a way of solving your problems and the suggestions below as clues to directions you might move. With this in mind, let's look at a random list of leadership problems.

APATHY

People express apathy in different ways. They seem disinterested during group discussions. They do not participate in group activities. They come late, are frequently absent, leave early. They do not volunteer to take responsibility or do not follow through on responsibilities they are assigned.

Apathy usually comes from a sense of powerlessness or lack of self-esteem. Apathetic group members feel that what they say or do will not make any difference. They may be attending the group because they are pressured to do so by parents and find no personal satisfaction in the group's activities. Or they may not know very many persons in the group and are afraid to risk being rejected if they make a suggestion. They do not feel a sense of ownership, that is, feel that it's *their* group. The group lacks a sense of community for them.

The first step in overcoming apathy is finding its cause. Ask for some feedback from group members on their feelings about the group. Make certain that they know that their feelings will be accepted and that they have the power to change the situation.

If apathy is a problem with the majority of your group members, you might ask everyone to complete open-ended statements anonymously. Use statements such as the following:

I come to this group because . . .
In this group I enjoy . . .
The people in this group are . . .
I wish this group would . . .
What I want most from this group is . . .
If I could change one thing in this group, I would . . .

If only two or three members seem apathetic, you may wish to talk individually with them about their feelings in relation to the group.

When you have collected information on the causes of apathy, let the group help you find ways to change the situation. If the group goals are not meeting their needs, set new goals. If only a few persons are making decisions, help the group become more democratic. If your leadership style is a problem, ask the group to help you change. Plan activities in which everyone can be involved. Provide the group with good problem-solving methods so it can work together on the group goals.

Do not respond to apathy by setting rigid standards (everyone must be here by eight o'clock; if you don't participate in a discussion, you'll be asked to do an extra assignment; only members who attend ten sessions in a row can go on our trip). Also, avoid responding to apathy by looking for more "inspiring" materials, more exciting activities, or a leader who is more entertaining. This may keep members coming, but it will not do anything to build a better group.

DISCIPLINE

Whole books have been written on discipline, and we cannot go into the subject in depth in these few pages. Instead, we will deal very briefly with some initial responses to discipline problems.

We become concerned about discipline when there are group members who break necessary rules, such as curfews at a conference center shared with other groups; when there is an intolerable amount of horseplay in a study group; or when others complain about the group's noise or behavior.

In order to maintain discipline, we must have clear and reasonable guidelines for behavior. These guidelines must be understood and accepted by the group. Some guidelines will be established for us by others, but if they are unreasonable, we should negotiate a change in them. (In one church, the junior highs were not permitted to use the church kitchen on Sunday night. Upon questioning this rule, they found that the custodian cleaned the kitchen after the morning coffee hour and didn't have time to clean it before a men's group met for breakfast the next morning. The rule was changed when the junior highs agreed to clean the kitchen before leaving on Sunday night.)

Other guidelines will be established to allow for maximum learning. Too much horseplay in a study group interferes with everyone's participation. Too much noise in your group may keep other groups meeting at the same time from functioning.

Try to keep the number of guidelines to a minimum. Too many rules are hard to remember and do not allow for much group flexibility. State any nonnegotiable guidelines at the beginning of any new group activity (a retreat, a trip, a new study group). Make sure everyone understands what they are. Then ask the group to decide on any additional guidelines which will help them function. The group should agree on their own guidelines right from the beginning.

When problems arise, deal with them individually. I do not like to determine a standard punishment for breaking rules before the rules are broken. I like to get at the reason the rules were broken and then deal with the behavior in terms of its cause.

There are two exceptions to this principle. If certain behavior will result in legal consequences, the group should be aware of these consequences and you, as a leader, will be responsible for the enforcement of legal regulations. Also, if property is damaged by a person in your group, the person should be held responsible for repairs or replacement.

In dealing with behavior problems, it is important to recognize that no one continues a behavior which does not bring some reward. Youth who engage in horseplay in a study group are getting more from the horseplay than from the study. To change their behavior, you will have to make the study more rewarding (perhaps it is not meeting any real needs of theirs) or not give them the attention they are seeking through horseplay (the attention is their reward; when it is not present, they may change their behavior).

At the same time, behavior which is disruptive to a group

cannot be tolerated. The whole group should not have to suffer because a few individuals are bored. So you will have to stop the behavior initially and then deal with its causes. Sometimes just asking the persons engaging in horseplay to stop will be enough. If they continue, you may have to ask them to leave the group and meet with you at a separate time to discuss the problem.

Always meet with individuals to discuss their behavior problems if the behavior continues or if it is a serious infraction of the rules. When you meet with them, discuss how their behavior affects *you*. Use what Thomas Gordon calls "I statements."[1] This will give them a chance to respond with some of their own reasons for behaving in the way they did—or at least to see the effect of their behavior. For example, let's say you're meeting with a young person who brought alcohol to your weekend retreat:

You: We set guidelines for this retreat, and one was that we would have no alcohol. I'm put in a very bad position if someone brings alcohol. The parents expect me to enforce this rule. If word gets back that three of our group were drunk on Friday night, we may have problems getting parents to agree to another retreat. Besides, it's illegal for youth under eighteen to drink alcohol in this state, and I could be held legally responsible if one of you were injured while under the influence of alcohol.

Youth: Yeah, I guess it is a problem for you.

You: Were you aware of the rule when you brought the beer along?

Youth: Sure, we went over the rules last week, and I got the letter everyone else got.

You: How did you feel about the rule?

Youth: Well, I knew it was necessary, but we always take beer to our parties, and I didn't see how we could have a good time out here in the woods without beer.

You: You think beer is necessary in order to have a good time?

Youth: Yeah, you know, when you get high, well, things just seem better.

You: Have you ever had a good time without beer—say before you began drinking beer?

Youth: Oh, sure, when I was younger. I mean, just joking around and playing games and things.

---

[1]"I statements" are statements in which you describe your feelings about a problem situation, allowing the person involved in the problem to respond to your needs rather than defend their own behavior, putting themselves into a win-lose situation. See *Teacher Effectiveness Training* by Thomas Gordon (New York: Peter H. Wyden, Inc., 1975).

You: Do you think there is a way you could have a good time here and still not put me on the spot?

Youth: Well, maybe if we had more things going on late at night—like if we could stay up until one o'clock looking at old movies or something.

In the above situation, you have helped a person change her or his behavior—to see that it is possible to have a good time without alcohol. If you had simply punished the behavior, you would have alienated the person from the group and perhaps even made her or him into a martyr in the eyes of the others who participated in the party, thus reinforcing the person's taking the risk of breaking the rules in other situations.

As mentioned previously, there are times when punishment must be used, especially when the rule breaking is serious and there are legal consequences or when property is damaged. When punishment is necessary, make sure everyone is aware of what the punishment will be before the rule is broken.

I usually do not like to ask youth to determine the punishment for specific behaviors. They are often very harsh on their peers. However, if a number of persons in the group are involved in breaking a rule, they may all share in a discussion of alternative behavior. Or, if the rule breaking affects the life of the total group, the whole group may want to discuss the problem together.

I also do not like to throw the problem of punishment onto parents. They are embarrassed if their child breaks a rule and may overreact with a stiff penalty. However, parents should be alerted to any serious behavior problems.

The objective in all discipline problems is to help youth practice new behavior because they find it rewarding, not because they fear the punishment someone will impose if they misbehave. Keeping this in mind, you should be able to find ways to solve many of your discipline problems.

MOTIVATION

How do we get youth interested in studying something serious? How can we get our group to be "spiritual"? How can we get them to be interested in service to others outside the group? These questions are often heard in church groups and they all relate to the same problem: motivation.

Persons are motivated to do the things which meet their needs or bring them satisfaction. Let's look at the problem of serious study, for example. As we pointed out earlier, youth are asking serious questions and spend many hours debating these with their friends. If a church group is dealing with the questions about which they are concerned, and if the group allows them room to consider many alternative answers to these questions, they will be motivated to discuss them in the group. Use an interest finder (such as the one given in the Appendix, page 118) to discover which questions are important to your youth. Then select subjects to study in which the majority of the group are interested.

Getting the group to be "spiritual" also involves meeting needs. Most youth have deep religious feelings and many have deep religious experiences. However, these are private experiences which may not be shared even with best friends. It is difficult to talk about them. There is always the fear that someone will laugh or consider them "weird." Youth are especially reluctant to share these experiences in a group unless that group is nonjudgmental—a place in which they feel secure and can share deeply. Only this kind of group can be authentically spiritual.

Service to persons outside the group is another area in which meeting needs is key. Many youth are too wrapped up in internal struggles to have the energy to be concerned about other people. They are trying to establish their identity, to develop self-confidence, to find a place for themselves in their peer society. This takes time and energy. Only when they have resolved some of these questions will they be able to think about others and respond to their needs.

The maturity of a group is also a factor in service outside the group, as we mentioned in the section on group development, page 64. When a group has become cohesive and stable, it is free to move outside itself to minister to others.

If you are faced with problems of motivation relating to any of the above areas, consider what needs are not being met and what might be wrong with the climate of your group.

ADULT COOPERATION

Many youth groups are limited in their effectiveness because adults in the church do not support them. Church boards may fail to appropriate money for their activities or allow them to earn money on their own. Parents may criticize some of their activities. Adult classes may take over the best rooms, leaving the basement for "the kids." Youth may not be asked to take any serious responsibility in the church.

Communication is the key to solving this problem. You may have to be the youth advocate with church boards. You may have to plan several meetings with parents to interpret the youth program as well as send letters to the homes explaining each new event. Youth may have to negotiate with other members of the church for rooms which will meet their needs.

A caution should be raised here. The important words in seeking adult cooperation in youth ministry are *communication* and *negotiation*. You should not let yourself get into a rigid position of always "sticking up for the youth," even though you are their advocate. You should not have to "take sides" when a dispute arises between adults and youth. Your role is to communicate the feelings of youth, or enable youth to communicate their own feelings, and then enable both adults and youth to negotiate solutions.

Youth ministry is a concern of the total church. To keep church members alert to this, you will have to keep them informed and involved. This is part of your role as a youth leader. You may find others in the church who are willing to work with you as advocates for youth. Welcome their support.

CLIQUES

Some groups develop small subgroups who enjoy each other's company to the exclusion of others. They may be a subgroup which has power in the larger group—the officers or the planning committee. They may be a subgroup who are looked down on by the rest of the group members—the outsiders.

These subgroups, or cliques, become very close friends, perhaps doing things together outside the group meetings. They may give their group a name, dress alike, or always arrive or leave together. They are a closed group, not letting anyone else into their circle.

Cliques can be very disruptive to groups. Inevitably they cause some people to feel left out. These people may lose interest in the group, feel powerless when they are there, or be argumentative or sullen. You cannot have a caring, redemptive group if you have cliques.

Cliques are generally made up of people who feel insecure individually. They need acceptance in a small group to feel they are worthwhile. Or they form when the total group does not offer adequate opportunity for personally satisfying participation.

To prevent cliques from forming, you will have to work on

making the total group an accepting, caring group. You will have to affirm each individual and help each person make a contribution to the group life.

If cliques do form, you will have to work on changing the negative effects they have on the group. Encourage the cliques to be concerned about group members who are feeling left out. Try to help them take more responsibility for the life of the total group. Divide the large group into subgroupings that encourage members of cliques to work with persons not in their cliques. Evaluate as a total group how much members feel a sense of belonging.

If the total group has become a clique, making new members feel unwelcome, confront them with the same kinds of concerns with which you confronted subgroups in the larger group. Help them move beyond stage three to stage four of group development.

SUMMARY

This chapter has touched very briefly on some common problems that face most leaders at one time or another: apathy, discipline, motivation, lack of adult cooperation, and cliques.

We have suggested that apathy comes from a sense of powerlessness or lack of self-esteem. It can be overcome by first finding its cause and helping apathetic group members label the cause, then by enabling group members to change the group so that it becomes one in which they have a voice, one in which they are working on goals which are important to them, and a group in which they seem to have a significant role.

Discipline problems arise because persons are having needs met through behavior which is unacceptable or illegal. In order to change this behavior, you will need to help the person find alternative ways of meeting his or her needs and develop self-discipline. You can cut down on discipline problems by stating clear guidelines for behavior, keeping guidelines to a minimum, and letting the group determine any guidelines which it feels are necessary to get its task accomplished. When behavior problems do arise, deal with them individually. Help the individual see how her or his behavior is affecting others, including yourself as leader. Help the person take responsibility for changing this behavior.

Motivation is a problem when a group is not meeting real needs. To deal with lack of motivation, determine what needs are not being met. Also, you may want to look at the climate of your group to determine whether it is open to persons expressing their real needs, their thoughts, and their feelings.

Cooperation of parents and other adults in the youth ministry program can be accomplished by concentrating on communicating your objectives in youth ministry with adults and by negotiating solutions to any problems which may arise between adults and youth. You may find a number of other adults who are willing to work with you in this advocacy role. And you can encourage youth to negotiate some solutions on their own.

Cliques develop in groups which do not offer adequate opportunity for personally satisfying participation or among youth who feel individually insecure and need acceptance in a small group to feel worthwhile. Cliques can be very disruptive to a group, but can also have some positive value if you can help them move to the mature phase of group life where they express concern for others outside their small group. To prevent cliques from forming, affirm each individual in the group and help each person make a contribution to the group life. If cliques do form, help them understand the negative effect they may be having on the total group and encourage them to take more responsibility for the life of the total group.

We have only covered a few of the many problems you may run into in youth leadership, and have given only broad suggestions for dealing with these problems. However, from this discussion, you may be able to discover some guidelines for dealing with such problems on your own: first, discover what caused the problem; then find several alternative ways of solving the problem, choosing the one or ones which seem to have the most chance of succeeding with your group. Experience will be your best ally in dealing with leadership problems. The more problems you handle successfully, the more confident you will be as you face new problems. No one can give you a pat solution for every situation you will face; you will have to experiment until you come up with your own solutions.

12 | Realistic Expectations of Youth Leadership

We began this book by stating that we need to be realistic about the kind of time and the kind of training a lay leader can devote to youth ministry. We will end it by looking at some realistic results a lay leader might expect in youth leadership.

LEARNING EXPERIENCES

Most church learning experiences are fringe experiences for youth. The one-hour class on Sunday morning, the two-hour youth meeting, even the weekend retreat four times a year or the week-long conference involve very little time when compared with the five days a week youth spend in school or the two to four hours a day they watch television.

You should not expect youth to become accomplished biblical scholars or expert theologians in this limited time. However, you can expect them to discover that the Bible has meaning for their lives, to understand basic Christian beliefs, and to formulate some viable Christian values. You can expect them to begin the lifelong journey of Christian discipleship. You can help them develop the skills to explore the Christian faith on their own as they move into adulthood.

GROUP DEVELOPMENT

The kind of group you are able to develop will again depend on the kind of time you have available and the kinds of opportunities you are able to provide. Actually, many churches have a high degree of success in developing groups which are caring and which reach out to serve others.

If you are able to meet in some large time blocks with your group (on retreats or trips or summer conferences), if you are able to have informal times with them as well as meet with them for learning experiences, if you develop skill in group leadership, you should be able to develop a group in which youth experience Christian community and are involved in mission as the servant church.

INDIVIDUAL GROWTH

Because individuals in your group will respond differently to your leadership and because your relationships with them will vary, the individual growth of members of your group is probably the area in which you will be least able to define your expectations.

You will seldom be able to see the kind of individual growth and change that you can "measure" at the end of the year. However, your influence will be felt in varying degrees in the lives of the members of your group.

Some of this influence may not be immediately evident. I have had youth tell me years after I worked with them as teenagers about an important change in their lives that occurred through some interaction in a group in which I was involved. At the time, I was completely unaware that anything significant was happening to anyone.

You should expect to see some individual growth among members of your group, but the growth you see is not indicative of all that God is doing in a person's life.

LEADER GROWTH

What about your own growth as leaders? Most of us need to keep growing or we lose interest in our task and feel frustrated at the level of our accomplishment.

You should not become discouraged because you lack the skills of some professional youth leaders who have had intensive specialized training. As a nonprofessional, you can continue to develop more and more skill each year you serve as a youth leader. You can take advantage of training opportunities offered by your denomination or region. You can enroll in skill courses in a nearby college. You can keep up-to-date on new developments in Christian education by subscribing to journals and church leader magazines.

Most important, you can learn from your own mistakes and successes. One of the best ways of doing this is to keep a journal of your experiences in youth leadership. Jot down a few notes after each group meeting. Take time to go over in your own mind what happened—to define ways in which you might have done things differently, to isolate problems and try to come up with solutions to these problems.

This reflection will help you to articulate your successes and failures and enable you to learn from them. (We do not learn by making mistakes; we learn by reflecting on why we made mistakes or why we succeeded.)

A SUPPORT GROUP

As you struggle to develop skills in youth leadership, it is helpful to have a support group from which you can gain strength, evaluation of your efforts, and comfort when you fail. This support group should be made up of your peers—perhaps others involved in youth leadership or in the teaching ministry of the church. It should meet regularly and concentrate on giving support to members as they carry out their leadership responsibilities.

Your support group may be involved in learning new leadership skills, but it should not meet solely for that purpose. It should be a place where you can ventilate your frustration, knowing it will be held in confidence; where you can learn from the experience of others; where you can share your own successes and rejoice with others at theirs.

If you are working as part of a team of teachers or youth counselors, the others on your team may be your support group. If you have sole responsibility for a youth group, you will need to seek support from persons related to other groups in the church.

Everyone needs someone on whom to rely for encouragement and realistic evaluation. Youth leaders are no exception. Find a group you can trust and lean on them. You'll find your job is much easier and more rewarding.

SUMMARY

This book has provided a framework for your step-by-step development as a youth leader. The potential for building on this framework is limited only by the time you have available and your own motivation.

The result will be a ministry with youth that has the kind of meaning the author of the following poem found as she reflected on her experience with the adult counselors of her senior high group:

This Was Just a Place of Passing[1]

This was just a place of passing,
A necessary step to be taken
To reach the higher goals.
You were just friends of passing,
The necessary love
To carry me to new love.

But then I look at your faces
And I think of the tears and the laughter—
Both you gave me.
And how I heard your words,
Filled with insight and confusion—
Both they made me
Into what I am now.

I am, now,
Not afraid to reach out
And touch a stranger
And make him my friend.
I am, now,
Much more ready
To accept myself
For what I really am.

I only wish now
I could tell you how I love you,
And hope that I gave you
All you gave to me
And tell you.

This is not just a place of passing
But a very special part of my life.
I will thank you.
You are not just friends of passing
But the loves of my life.
I will remember you.

—Shannon Kille

[1]Reprinted with permission from *Baptist Leader*, August, 1975.

Appendix

SAMPLE LEADER CONTRACTS

The following are sample contracts which might be prepared for positions of youth leadership in the church. See the reference to these contracts on page 11.

SAMPLE CHURCH SCHOOL TEACHER CONTRACT

POSITION: Ninth Grade Church School Teacher
RESPONSIBILITIES:
  Teach the ninth grade class for one semester (September to January).
  Enable the students to understand the study material as completely as possible.
  Encourage students to help plan class sessions and to take an active part in leading these sessions.
  Evaluate with students their growth in relation to the course objectives.
  Keep a record of the attendance of class members, and call any who are absent more than two Sundays in a row.
  Attend teacher meetings as called.
  Attend meetings of the total youth ministry staff as called.
  Participate in leader development sessions as required.
  Notify the church school superintendent of any class sessions you must miss.
TIME COMMITMENT:
  At least one hour preparation for class each week.
  One hour class session each Sunday.
  Approximately twelve hours of meetings and/or training sessions per semester.

Signed_____Date_____

SAMPLE YOUTH GROUP COUNSELOR CONTRACT

POSITION: Youth Group Counselor
RESPONSIBILITIES:

Meet once a week with the youth group for a two-hour meeting.

Meet with the group members at other times for retreats, individual counseling, social events.

Meet periodically with the group or a committee from the group for planning. Help the group set goals, plan activities, and find resources.

Periodically evaluate with the group how well they have met their goals.

Provide information to the total church about the group's activities.

Meet with parents periodically to answer their questions about the group's goals and activities.

Participate in leader development events as required.

Participate in leader meetings as called.

Notify youth coordinator when you cannot be present.

TIME COMMITMENT:

Two hours per week for group meeting.

Two to four weekends per year for retreats.

Unspecified number of days for special sessions (planning meetings, parties, counseling, etc.). Number of days to be determined by counselor's available time and youth group needs.

Approximately twelve hours per semester for training and leader meetings.

Signed_____Date_____

SAMPLE INTEREST FINDERS

Here are two types of ways to gather information about subjects your group might be interested in exploring. (See the reference to these on pages 56 and 108.)

AN INTEREST QUESTIONNAIRE

Instructions: First, go through the questionnaire and place a check mark in front of each subject that interests you. Then go back and place a star beside each subject that is of *special* interest to you.

1. ___ Cheating in school.
2. ___ Getting along with parents.
3. ___ How to budget the money I earn.

4. ___ Failure.
5. ___ New ways to worship.
6. ___ Busing to achieve racial integration.
7. ___ The energy crisis.
8. ___ Being more open in our group.
9. ___ Fighting with brothers and sisters.
10. ___ Answering questions about sex.
11. ___ Problem drinking.
12. ___ Being more involved in decision making in our church.
13. ___ Having my parents trust me more.
14. ___ Getting along better with people at school.
15. ___ Finding some purpose in life.
16. ___ How police treat youth in our town.
17. ___ The lack of respect youth show for teachers.
18. ___ Vandalism in our town.
19. ___ My physical growth.
20. ___ Boredom at school.
21. ___ Communicating better at home.
22. ___ Freedom of our school newspaper.
23. ___ How to pray.
24. ___ Pollution in our town.
25. ___ Finding what the Bible means today.
26. ___ Being able to use the family car.
27. ___ Pressure to get good grades.
28. ___ Having more freedom.
29. ___ Using drugs.
30. ___ Having adults in the church listen to youth more.

Note to Leader: Collate the questionnaires by listing in one column all items which were checked, with the number of checks each received. In a second column list all items which were starred and the number of times they were starred.

Rank both columns by placing a "one" before the items checked or starred the most times, a "two" before the next highest checks and stars, etc.

If the same item is ranked highest in both columns, that is the item to study. If the columns differ, decide whether you want to study the item that most people checked or the item starred as most important.

After the subjects have been ranked, you will have to develop a clear understanding about what the problem areas selected mean to each person. For example, if a number of people marked

"Being more open in our group," ask them to give examples of what they would like to happen in the group and examples (anonymously) of times when the group did not seem open. Also, you may wish to replace some of the question areas above with subjects which are of more immediate concern to your group.

A Ladder of Concern

Draw a ladder, like the sample given below, on the chalkboard. Ask everyone to copy the ladder on a sheet of paper. At the top of the ladder, write the words "strong feelings—pro or con." At the bottom, write "weak feelings—pro or con." Develop a number of statements like the samples given here which deal with areas about which members of your group might be concerned. Underline a key word in each statement. Ask group members to write the key word in a spot on the ladder which corresponds to their feelings about the statement. If they feel **strongly,** they should place the word at the top of the ladder; if they have very **weak** feelings about the statement, they should place the word at the bottom; if their feelings are **in-between** (neither very strong nor very weak), they should place the word in the middle.

Sample Statements

Strong feelings—
pro or con.

Weak feelings—
pro or con.

1. Parents should <u>trust</u> their teenagers more.
2. Most of my friends use <u>drugs</u>.
3. The <u>Bible</u> is a difficult book to read.
4. It's hard to know how to deal with <u>sex</u> these days.
5. Our <u>church</u> doesn't care what the youth think.
6. <u>TM</u> is replacing prayer for many people.
7. Going to <u>college</u> doesn't make sense anymore.
8. People should use less <u>energy</u>.
9. There should be more <u>jobs</u> for youth.
10. <u>Women</u> should earn the same pay as men for similar jobs.

The items which most people place at the top of the ladder are the ones about which there is the most interest in your group.

CREATING A SIMULATION GAME

There are many simulation games available, but a group can sometimes learn more by developing their own. (See "Simulation Games," page 74). One of the easiest ways of creating your own game is to adapt an existing recreational game like Monopoly or checkers to achieve an educational objective.

The following is an example of how this can be done with the game Twister. This game helps to illustrate the power of cliques.

School Survival[1]

Tape to the floor a large piece of plastic, the size of a playing sheet for Twister. Draw a pyramid on the sheet. Ask the group to divide the pyramid into the various cliques in their school, with the clique having the most status on top and the lowest on the bottom. (For example, the socialites might be on top and the greasers on the bottom. Use names of cliques that are common in your school.) Write the names of the cliques on the pyramid.

Ask members of the group to write on 3" x 5" cards the things a person must do or become in order to get into each clique (make the football team, throw the best parties, have the highest average in math, etc.). On separate cards, write what a person might do to be expelled from each clique (be dropped from the team, fail math); be sure to include the name of the clique on the card. Shuffle each set of cards and stack in separate piles: one pile for the joining activities and one for the expelling activities. Find a spinner dial from a game like Twister and cover the colors or numbers with a piece of paper. On the top half of the paper covering the dial, print "join" and on the bottom half print "lose."

To play the game, divide the group into two teams. Each team chooses one person to spin the dial. Teams take turns in spinning. If the pointer stops in the "join" area, the "spinner" takes a card from the set that tells what a person must do to get into a certain clique. The team has two minutes to decide if someone from their team wants to do what the card says and join the clique. The person who joins the clique stands in the area for that clique on the pyramid. If no one stands on the sheet, the "spinner" must select a card from the "lose" pile. He or she must hold the "lose" card until a member of his/her team is in the clique referred to on the card, and then this person automatically loses his/her place in that clique. (The "spinner" should not tell the rest of the team

[1]Adapted from "School Survival Weekend" in *Youth Plus*, a supplement to *Youth Magazine* (Philadelphia: United Church Press, October, 1976).

members what is on the "lose" card. They are to show it when a fellow team member joins the clique to which it refers.)

The game is played until all cards are used. The team with the most members on the pyramid at that time wins. The group members then discuss what it feels like to be in a clique they have chosen or to be excluded from a clique.

GROUP GROWTH EXERCISES

The following experiences can be used to help group members communicate more effectively, become better acquainted, and relate more easily with one another. The specific uses are identified in each exercise. (See chapter 7 for times these exercises might be needed.)

Shoe Sharing

Purpose: To help group members become better acquainted.

Procedure: Ask all group members to take off their shoes and throw them into the center of the room. Divide the group into pairs. Ask one member of each pair to describe themselves in such a way that their partner can find their shoes. They will not describe their shoes, but will say, for example, "I am very practical" or "I follow the latest fashions." The partners then look for shoes in the pile until they find their partner's shoes. Then the other member of the pair describes her or his shoes and the partner looks for these shoes in the pile. Spend time discussing how clothing helps us tell others something about ourselves.

Mirror

Purpose: To understand how persons lead and follow.

Procedure: The exercise is done without talking. Divide the group into pairs. Ask each pair to face each other. Begin playing a recording of orchestral music. At a signal from you, one person in each pair will begin moving in time to the music (not dancing, but making motions with hands, walking around the room, etc.). The partners do not decide who will begin moving—one person simply begins. The other person does exactly what the partner is doing, acting like a mirror to this person. At another signal from you, partners switch places and the follower becomes the leader. Discuss how it feels to be both a leader and a follower.

Blind Walk

Purpose: To develop trust in another person.

Procedure: Divide the group into pairs. Blindfold one member of each pair. Partners then lead the blindfolded members around a room or around a section of the out-of-doors. At a given signal, remove the blindfolds and place them on the persons who were leading. Repeat the exercise. At the end of the time period, talk about how it feels to have to trust another person.

Giving Gifts

Purpose: To affirm something positive about each individual.

Procedure: Tape a piece of paper on each person's back. Ask members of the group to take pencils, mill around the group, and write on the pieces of paper the gifts they feel each person has to give. When everyone has finished, ask each group member to look at the pieces of paper from his/her back. Have them add any other gifts they think they have to offer.

Sewing a Group

Purpose: To express, symbolically, the closeness of a group.

Procedure: Seat the group in a tight circle. Give one member a large ball of yarn. Ask this person to tie the end of the yarn around her or his wrist and toss the ball to someone else. This person wraps the yarn around herself or himself and tosses the ball to someone else. Eventually the group is "sewn" together. Discuss how well this illustrates real closeness in the group.

Imaginary Ball Game

Purpose: To learn to communicate nonverbally.

Procedure: Arrange the group in a circle. Tell them that there is an imaginary ball in the center of the group. They can make the ball into any shape they wish—large, small, a balloon, a football, a tennis ball. They can play with the ball, but must not talk. At a given signal, the game begins. Without talking, one person should go to the center of the circle, pick up the ball, play with it, and throw it to another person. Play for about ten minutes. Then discuss what was communicated. Was anyone angry, happy, concerned, lonely? Point out how much we communicate without speaking.

Active Listening

Purpose: To understand the feelings behind verbal statements.

Procedure: Divide the group into pairs. Assign them a subject to talk about, such as a recent football game, school, the fellowship group, parents. One member of each pair makes a statement about the subject. The other member gives feedback, saying, "You feel _____about_____." For example, one member says, "I hate school more and more each day; it's a bore." The other person says, "You feel bored with school." The first person then responds with "yes" or "no" and goes on to another statement about the subject. The same procedure is repeated with the next and following statements. At a given signal, reverse roles. Then talk as a total group about the value of understanding feelings.

A PROCESS FOR PROBLEM SOLVING[2]

This process can help you understand exactly what your problem is, why it is not being solved, and how you can work toward solving it.

1. State the problem as clearly as possible in terms of what you would like to see happen. For example, if attendance is dropping off, your problem statement would be: To have more people attend the group.

2. Divide a piece of paper into two columns: A and B. (If using the process with a group, use newsprint or a chalkboard.) In column A, list all of the factors which keep you from solving the problem. For example, in the attendance problem given above, you might list: meeting time the same as school sports events, too much homework, parents not interested in the church, etc. In column B, list all of the factors which work toward helping you solve the problem. For example: youth who come seem excited about the group, group meets some needs not met in other groups, strong leadership in the group, etc.

3. Look at the two lists. Which factors in each list seem most important? Place a star beside these. Then, for each starred item in column A, brainstorm how you can eliminate this negative factor. For example, if your meeting time conflicts with a school event, can you change the time of your meeting? (In brainstorming, don't evaluate ideas—get all ideas out and then choose those that seem to be the most effective.) Then brainstorm how you can strengthen the positive factors starred in column B.

4. Choose the most effective ideas in each brainstorm list and develop a plan of action. Assign persons to carry out the action.

[2]Based on "A Problem-Solving Program" by Saul Eisen (Washington, D.C.: NTL Institute for Applied Behavioral Science. Associated with the National Education Association, 1201 Sixteenth Street, N.W., Washington, DC 20036.)

Resources

UNDERSTANDING YOUTH

Adolescence: Crisis or Opportunity. A film which deals with adolescent needs, especially in terms of finding identity. Interviews with a psychologist, a YMCA counselor, and a high school teacher focus on the role of the adult in relating to adolescents. Rental: $15.00 from Film Fair Communications, 10900 Ventura Boulevard, Studio City, CA 91604.

Communicating with Junior Highs by Robert Browning. How to listen to, learn from, and engage in dialogue with younger teens. $1.95. (Nashville: Abingdon Press, 1976)

Don't Be Afraid. A film which helps adults overcome apprehension about working with today's youth. Rental: $15.00 from American Baptist Films, Valley Forge, PA 19481.

Five Cries of Youth by Merton P. Strommen. The results of a survey of over 7,000 youth, church related and non-church related. $6.95. (Harper & Row, Publishers, 1974)

Gold Is the Way I Feel. A film in which youth comment on their world. Rental: $10.00 from American Baptist Films, Valley Forge, PA 19481.

I Am. In this film a young adolescent boy discovers that he is "somebody" by moving from a world of fantasy in which he assumes heroic roles to the real world where he discovers he doesn't have to be a hero to be important. Rental information from Wombat Productions, Inc., 77 Tarrytown Road, White Plains, NY 10607.

Teaching Early Adolescents Creatively: A Manual for Church School Teachers by Edward D. Seely. A manual which focuses on the church school class, but can be adapted for any setting. $2.95. (Philadelphia: The Westminster Press, 1971)

Young Girls: A Portrait of Adolescence by Gisela Konopka. A book based on extensive interviews with over one thousand girls. The material is organized by themes which were of central concern to the girls: life goals, sexuality, adults, friends, loneliness, drugs and alcohol, school, youth organizations, and social-political concerns. $2.95. (Englewood Cliffs, N.J.: Prentice-Hall, Inc., 1976)

Youth, World, and Church by Sara Little. Shows how youth, who are full members of the congregation, can become involved in the church's mission. $3.45. (Atlanta: John Knox Press, 1968)

PERIODICALS

Mass Media. Biweekly newsletter reviewing new resources, especially films and TV programs. Subscription, $10.00 per year. Order from: Mass Media, 2116 North Charles Street, Baltimore, MD 21218.

Probe. Newsletter about new resources and creative approaches to church and community work. Subscription, $5.00 per year. Order from: *Probe,* Christian Associates of Southwest Pennsylvania, 401 Wood St.; 1800 Arrott Bldg., Pittsburgh, PA 15222.

Scan. Monthly newsletter which evaluates new resources. Subscription, $6.00. Order from: *Scan,* P.O. Box 12811, Pittsburgh, PA 15241.

Cultural Information Service. In-depth reviews of books, films, TV programs, records—both secular and sacred. Subscription, $12.00 per year. Order from: Cultural Information Service, P.O. Box 92, New York, NY 10016.

LEADER SKILLS

Adventuring with Youth by Edwin Hinshaw. A loose-leaf notebook for the advanced adult worker with youth. Designed for "building a group in which each member is sensitive to needs, concerns, and feelings of the others." $4.95. (Richmond, Ind: Friends United Press, 1969)

Basic Bible Study for Teachers. A self-instructional filmstrip kit which trains teachers to identify key persons of the Old Testament, as well as to use basic Bible reference books. Filmstrip, cassette tape recording, leader's manual, participant's worksheets. $12.00 from Griggs Educational Service, P. O. Box 363, Livermore, CA 94550.

The Care and Counseling of Youth in the Church by Paul B. Irwin. Pulls together available information about youth ministry, stressing the needs for personalized relationships. Deals with the developmental and religious needs of youth today. $2.95. (Philadelphia: Fortress Press, 1975).

Developing the Art of Discussion by John Bushman and Sandy Jones. This is a handbook written to aid church school teachers in building discussion skills in their classes. $2.50. (Valley Forge: Judson Press, 1977)

Handbook of Structured Experiences for Human Relations Training. Five volumes, each containing a variety of individual and group growth experiences. $3.00 each. (La Jolla, Calif.: University Associates, Inc., 1972)

Introducing the Bible by William Barclay. Biblical theology for the average church member. This book covers the Old and New Testaments and Apocrypha. Comes with two cassette tapes for $9.95. Book without cassettes, $1.95. (Nashville: Abingdon Press, 1973)

40 Ways to Teach in Groups by Martha M. Leypoldt. A variety of teaching skills which can be used for group learning. $2.50. (Valley Forge: Judson Press, 1967)

The Joy of Learning. This filmstrip illustrates a learning center as a place where learners interact with each other and with selected resources and explores the roles of leaders, students, and learning environment. One side of the record gives an overview of the learning center approach and some of the elements involved in moving into this approach. Side two gives a more detailed explanation. $5.95 from American Baptist Films, Valley Forge, PA 19481.

Learning Through Simulation Games by Philip H. Gillispie. A listing of thirty simulation games under six content areas: freedom, life, peace, love, happiness, and communication. Several games are printed in their entirety. Describes how simulation games can be used and how to develop your own simulation game. $7.95. (New York: Paulist Press, 1974)

Raise a Jubilee by Donald F. Jensen. General resources for people

128   Creative Youth Leadership

involved in planning an overall ministry with music for junior highs. $5.25. (Nashville: Graded Press)

Retreat Handbook by Virgil and Lynn Nelson. Comprehensive handbook for planning retreats with many suggested program ideas for use with youth and adults. $5.95. (Valley Forge: Judson Press, 1976)

Shaping the Church's Ministry with Youth (revised) by David Evans. Urges a reexamination of the ministry with youth for evidence of overemphasis on organization and programming and encourages guiding youth in experiencing the realities of Christian living. $2.95. (Valley Forge: Judson Press, 1977)

T.E.T.: Teacher Effectiveness Training by Thomas Gordon. Communication skills for the teacher based on the author's highly successful model for parents, *Parent Effectiveness Training*. $9.95. (New York: Peter H. Wyden Inc., 1975)

Vacation Time, Leisure Time, Any Time You Choose by Mary Calhoun. A book of program ideas and administration suggestions for vacation/leisure education for the whole church. Includes chapters on camping, family activities, travel and tour, festivals, and a learning center. $2.25. (Nashville: Abingdon Press, 1976)

Youth Ministry: Sunday, Monday, and Every Day by John Carroll and Keith Ignatius. How to plan and administer a youth ministry program—from selecting a youth committee to evaluating results. $1.65. (Valley Forge: Judson Press, 1972)